Charles H McKenzie

The Religious Sentiments of Charles Dickens

Collected from His Writings

Charles H McKenzie

The Religious Sentiments of Charles Dickens
Collected from His Writings

ISBN/EAN: 9783744665025

Printed in Europe, USA, Canada, Australia, Japan

Cover: Foto ©Lupo / pixelio.de

More available books at **www.hansebooks.com**

THE RELIGIOUS SENTIMENTS

OF

Charles Dickens,

COLLECTED FROM HIS WRITINGS.

BY

CHARLES H. McKENZIE.

LONDON:
WALTER SCOTT, 14 PATERNOSTER SQUARE,
AND NEWCASTLE-UPON-TYNE.
1884.

CONTENTS.

	PAGE
Prefatory Remarks	5—8

CHAPTER I.

Two periods distinguishable in his Writings—His Religious Sentiments in his earlier books . . . . 9—17

CHAPTER II.

Prejudices removed and a proper spirit of impartial inquiry suggested—The hypocrites of Dickens . . . 18—41

CHAPTER III.

Dickens a true friend to approved Christian profession—His good clergymen . . . . 42—56

CHAPTER IV.

What he condemns and objects to in Religious Practice—The No-Popery Riots—Roman Catholicism . . 57—80

CHAPTER V.

What he objects to in Religious Practice (*continued*)—Abuses in the Church of England—Puritanism—Gloomy and austere Religion—The Jellyby-Pardiggle Missionary Zeal . . 81—96

CHAPTER VI.

Charles Dickens on Christian Doctrine—Immortality—God, the Creator, the Father, the Judge—The Resurrection 97—120

CHAPTER VII.

Charles Dickens on Christian Doctrine (*continued*)—The Atonement and the Person of Jesus Christ—The Fall of Man—Probation—Baptism—The Sabbath . 121—143

CHAPTER VIII.

Charles Dickens a Christian Advocate—The humanity of his Religion, and advocacy for the poor and downtrodden—Temperance Reform—Christian Evidences —A Tract . 144—163

CHAPTER IX.

On Charles Dickens's Use of the Scriptures and Scriptural Doctrines throughout his Works . . 164—171

PREFATORY REMARKS.

N commencing the congenial task before me, I should state the reasons which stimulated me to undertake it, and eventually to give its results to the world, for the one, at the outset, was independent of the other.

In the fulfilment of my whilom functions as a lay preacher of the gospel, I happened, one night, to bring some of the sentiments of Charles Dickens to bear upon the subject under exposition, which led to some slight discussion between an estimable lady and myself, in which she emphatically denied, and I asserted, that the great author had sound Christian views. Although feeling justified in my position in a general mental review of his writings, yet I felt unprepared to give the proofs to substantiate my assurance, having, indeed, to admit to myself that my opinion was formed by the general impression gained from simple reading, rather than from any passages retained in my memory sufficiently to the point to establish my conviction; yet that conviction was so strong, that, though a very distant chance of having to yield the battle to the fair may have qualified my assurances, I engaged to collect the evidence which would convince her.

It is needless to say, as an ardent disciple of him who has been termed the great master of his art, and as a humble but loving disciple of that Greater Master whom Charles Dickens delighted to honour, with what zest my voluntary task was entered upon. I have read the books many times in my life, and would have read them many times again, for mere gratification of myself and other people; but, naturally, the oft-told tale must lose the charm that once enhanced it, and I often thought, with regret, that the once almost boundless scope was becoming circumscribed to me, and that the keen relish must diminish with growing familiarity. How gladly, then, this motive was welcomed which enabled me once more to take up the beloved books, to read them all with a new and absorbing interest, in which I was gratified and astonished by the voluminous and positive evidence collected from every succeeding volume, and my original humble motive grew to be a more ambitious one.

Before much progress had been made I was

constrained to admit that, with all my admiration for these books, I had read them only superficially, and had, in that, done little short of an injustice to their writer. In my enjoyment of his mirth-provoking creations, and my admiration of his power of moving the heart by his pathos, I had been ever hurried breathlessly on in that enchanting whirl of excitement which he, of all men, possessed the power of surrounding his reader with, and had failed to mark those subtle touches by which the author, like the painter, establishes his genius. And I believe that most people do read them in the same spirit the first time, and carry away an imperfect, and, consequently, an unfair estimate of his real character, motives, and heart. So I was brought in my task to see that many admirers of the writings of Charles Dickens do not rightly appreciate the real worth of the man and his life-work, and, when they are anything more than amused and interested, do not often rise beyond the admission that he was a great social reformer and moralist, which a man may be, after all, without being a Christian, in its scriptural meaning.

The more clearly I saw this, and the more convinced I became of his true, clear, broad, and minutely-defined Christian views, the more the purpose that was forming in my mind grew, until it assumed the terms of a positive duty. This purpose was to do justice to the memory of Charles

Dickens by establishing, by those proofs which are so often overlooked, the fact of his vital religious character, which, though a fact, is so strangely ignored, misunderstood, and actually denied, in places.

I venture to dedicate the results of my pleasant task to my lady friend, for whose especial edification it was originally undertaken, and I offer it to the public with all its *de*merits upon its head, but with certainly *this* merit, of being a genuine Tribute to the Memory of Charles Dickens.

I beg to express my indebtedness to Messrs. CHAPMAN & HALL for their very generous permission to use the extracts which have been necessary to the completion of this volume.

C. H. McKENZIE.

The Religious Sentiments of Charles Dickens.

CHAPTER I.

Two Periods distinguishable in his Writings—His Religious Sentiments in his earlier Books.

CHARLES DICKENS was something more than a Novelist, though some of his admirers rise no higher in their estimate of him than by admitting that he was an exceptionally good one. He was even something more than a Moralist and a Reformer, to the perception of which his less frivolous readers rise. But it is doubtful whether he is much known as a Christian teacher, though the proof lies obviously and unequivocally throughout his writings. Many, perhaps most, earnest readers of these wonderful books feel all the better in their hearts after they *have* read, though they cannot, perhaps, readily detect the subtle touches by which they have been quickened. We are told that the working-out of the propositions of Euclid, in our school-days, unconsciously developes our logical faculties, and, even though they may afterwards be forgotten, and become a sealed book to us, they fulfil their part, and leave the evidences of their utility to endure throughout a lifetime. In just such a way is many a religious character imperceptibly formed by the elevating and moral influences around the child and the youth, which, though he may not appreciate them, nor participate in them with any keen delight, help to mould his future character, and to form impressions which, starting into vitality by the power of circumstances, he may be at a loss to account for the existence of, nor ever think, probably, of referring them to the power of the religious influence which he despised. In Dickens's own words, in so early a book as the *Sketches by Boz*—

"There are strange chords in the human heart, which will lie dormant through years of depravity and wickedness, but which will vibrate at last to some slight circumstance apparently trivial in itself, but connected by some undefined and indistinct association with past days that can never be recalled, and with bitter recollections, from which the most degraded creature in existence cannot escape." (Chapter xxxiii.)

It is not impossible that there may be some people (readers of Dickens's writings) conscious (I was going to say, troubled) by religious sentiments and religious forebodings in their minds, who wonder how they got there, and who would be very much astonished could they trace them to the influence of Dickens. Be it my pleasant province to endeavour to lead them to that possible contingency. At any rate, I have the confidence that I shall be permitted to demonstrate to some who repudiate, to convince some who doubt, yet hope, and to establish the convictions of many who think that the religious sentiments of Dickens were those of a regenerate and enlightened Christian man, who, as such, may have fulfilled the highest duty of Christianity in evidencing, inclining towards, and building up souls in the truth of God, and of His Son Jesus Christ our Redeemer.

I ask no one to receive this, my distinct conviction, upon my own bare assurance; but ask all to impartially and honestly consider the evidence patiently collected, and now submitted upon its own merits.

I would beg leave, in the first place, to note a certain distinction. We are taught, by our Christian religion, that there was a period in the history of every regenerate soul when spiritual life became raised from the grave of natural depravity, and was quickened into a vitality and a heavenly knowledge, which the man, however wise and moral, never possessed before. If we look for the evidences of such a change in the subject of our consideration (and he speaks of such a change as involved in religion, as I shall have an opportunity to point out afterwards), I ask if it may not be plainly discerned at a certain epoch in his writings?

His books appear to divide themselves into two distinct classes. While throughout them all there runs the rich exuberance of his humour and descriptive power, and that rare vein of pathos for which he was so famous; and while the pledged Reformer stands out uncompromisingly from an early period, and before the presumable change, yet there is a certain something in the succeeding books not so obvious in the first few. And I may as well, in this place, mark the division. The *Sketches by Boz*, the *Pickwick Papers*, *Oliver Twist*, and *Nicholas Nickleby* form the first group; following which, *The Old Curiosity Shop* and *Barnaby Rudge*, under the original collective title of *Master Humphrey's Clock*, head the list of the works of the latter and more earnest period of his career as an author.

Who will compare, carefully and critically, the last book of the first batch and the first book of the last batch, and not mark the great difference of the spirit which breathes throughout their serious parts? *Nicholas Nickleby*, like the three books which preceded it, is full of rollicking fun, and designed, in a great measure, to amuse, truly ; but there are very serious parts in its plot where opportunity occurs for that sound morality and religious sentiment by which *all* his latter works are characterised. The deaths of Godfrey and Ralph Nickleby, the children of Dotheboys Hall, the story of Madeline Bray, and the characters of Kate, Smike, and the Cheeryble Brothers, afford vehicles for the introduction of very elevated sentiments. Not that they are totally wanting, but there is not the ring about them that we find he makes of such opportunities in his following writings, and they are just such remarks, suggested by the necessities for preserving the unities of the situation and the relevancy of the characters, as any man, with a respect for religion, without its quickened appreciation, might be supposed to make.

For example, Godfrey Nickleby, in dying, commends his widow and orphans to the care of One who never deserted the widow or her fatherless children (chapter i.). Cheeryble says, "Thank God," lifts off his hat and looks grave, speaks of the wisdom of heavenly decrees, and describes himself to Ralph Nickleby as "an erring and imperfect man ;" but he is also slightly given to saying "Damn," although he is described as "earnest and guileless."

The death of Smike has some of that spiritual fervour and pathos about it which hallows so many of those most pathetic passages in his writings, and bears witness to his confidence in immortality :—

"'I am not afraid to die,' he said. 'I am quite contented. I almost think that if I could rise from this bed quite well, I should not wish to do so now. You have so often told me we shall meet again—so very often lately, and now I feel the truth of that so strongly—that I can even bear to part from you.'"

. . . . . .

"He fell into a slight slumber, and waking, smiled as before ; then spoke of beautiful gardens, which, he said, stretched out before him, and were filled with figures of men, women, and many children, all with light upon their faces ; then whispered that it was Eden—and so died." (Chapter lix.)

If these sentiments are not acceptable evidence of his own feelings, seeing they are identified with the character of a half-witted lad, I hasten to supplement them by a quotation from an earlier chapter, suggested by the description of the approaching end of Smike, which are obviously the sentiments of the author himself :—

"There is a dread disease . . . in which the struggle between soul and body is so gradual, quiet, and solemn, and the result so sure that, day by day, and grain by grain, the mortal part wastes and withers away, so that the spirit grows light and sanguine with its lightening load, and *feeling immortality at hand*, deems it but a new term of mortal life." (Chapter xlix.)

Beyond this there is little in *Nicholas Nickleby* which can be adduced as evidence in support of the argument; but now turn to *The Old Curiosity Shop*, and do no more than scan its pages, and mark how they teem with assurances of immortality, faith in God, teachings of the fall of human nature, and the existence of heaven and its angels, all of which will be quoted hereafter in their proper places. Read especially the death of Little Nell, and say if ever the words were penned, in such connection throughout, where there breathes more spiritual a fervour, more faithful a hope, more exalted a trust in that which is not of this world, as there is here? It seems as though here were those early ascriptions of devotion which inspire a lately quickened soul, and which urge it to "tell its raptures all abroad ;" and how natural that the great author, if that be true which is surmised, should choose such a medium as this to gratify that propensity awakened within him.

Taking this view, which is not, however, advanced as incontestable, I shall ask to be permitted to base my estimate of the religious character of Charles Dickens upon those of his writings which are initiated by *The Old Curiosity Shop*, or *Master Humphrey's Clock*, as that is more legitimately the threshold. It is but fair that we should judge the Christianity of a man by his profession since he became a Christian, and though I shall refer, from time to time, to his earlier writings, the evidence shall be mainly taken from the latter. I presume that what the strictest critic will require will be to ascertain whether Charles Dickens was a Christian writer at any time, and will not be so hyper-critical as to dispute the point if there is not sufficient evidence in his *earlier* works.

But before relegating these earlier works to the debatable land assigned to them, let me make a few quotations from the remainder of them, to add to the foregoing extracts from *Nicholas Nickleby*.

In the "Visit to Newgate" he tells of a condemned felon there, who,

"Now that the illusion (of reprieve) is at last dispelled, now that eternity is before him and guilt behind, now that his fears of death amount almost to madness, and an overwhelming sense of his helpless, hopeless state rushes upon him, is lost and stupefied, and has neither thoughts to turn to, nor power to call upon the Almighty Being, from whom alone he can seek mercy and forgiveness, and before whom his repentance can alone avail." (*Sketches by Boz*, chapter xxv.)

In the harrowing tale of "The Drunkard's Death" the following words are put into the mouth of his accusing son :—

"My brother's blood and mine is on your head; I never had kind look, or word, or care from you, and, alive or dead, I never will forgive you. Die when you will, or how, I will be with you. I speak as a dead man now, and I warn you, father, that as surely as you must one day stand before your Maker, so surely shall your children be there, hand in hand, to cry for judgment against you." (*Sketches by Boz.*)

The following testimony to the power of prayer closes the tale of the "Black Veil":—

"In the transient gleam of recollection and consciousness which preceded her death, a prayer for his (the surgeon's) welfare and protection, as fervent as mortal ever breathed, rose from the lips of this poor friendless creature. The prayer flew to heaven and was heard. The blessings he was instrumental in conferring have been repaid to him a thousand-fold." (*Sketches by Boz.*)

From *Oliver Twist*:—

"' Heaven will never let her die so young,' said Oliver.

"' Hush!' said Mrs. Maylie. 'You think like a child, poor boy. But you teach me my duty, notwithstanding. . . . I have seen enough to know that it is not always the youngest and best who are spared to those that love them; but this should give us comfort in our sorrow; for Heaven is just; and such things teach us, impressively, that there is a brighter world than this; and that the passage to it is speedy. God's will be done! I love her; and He knows how well.'"

. . . . . .

"'What of Rose?' cried the old lady. 'Tell me at once! . . . in the name of heaven!'

"'You must compose yourself,' said the doctor, supporting her. 'Be calm, my dear ma'am, pray.'

"'Let me go, in God's name! My dear child! She is dead! she is dying!'

"'No!' cried the doctor, passionately. 'As He is good and merciful, she will live to bless us all, for years to come.'

"The lady fell upon her knees, and tried to fold her hands

together; but the energy which had supported her so long fled up to heaven with her first thanksgiving." (Chapter xxxiii.)

"Without strong affection and humanity of heart, and gratitude to that Being whose code is mercy, and whose great attribute is benevolence to all things that breathe, happiness can never be attained."

. . . .

"If the spirits of the dead ever come back to earth, to visit spots hallowed by the love—the love beyond the grave—of those whom they knew in life, I believe that the shade of Agnes sometimes hovers round that solemn nook. I believe it none the less because that nook is in a church, and she was weak and erring." (Chapter liii.)

We must not pass over the sentiment which he puts into the mouth of Rose Maylie, when she tells Nancy that "it is never too late for penitence and atonement" (chapter xl.); and we may conclude our gatherings from *Oliver Twist* by the words concluding the description of Nancy's cruel death :—

"Raising herself, with difficulty, on her knees, she drew from her bosom a white handkerchief, and holding it up, in her folded hands, as high towards heaven as her feeble strength would allow, breathed one prayer for mercy to her Maker." (Chapter xlviii.)

Even from that mad revel, the *Pickwick Papers*, we are able to select the following :—

"Heaven forgive me the supposition, if it is an uncharitable one." "The Bible was kept as carefully as ever." " . . . and fervently besought the Almighty Being." "Her sorrows were known to man, her virtues to God." " . . . the commandment he had reverenced as a child, and forgotten as a man." (From the story of "The Convict's Return," in chapter vi.)

In the same book, the cobbler reads the Bible to the dying legatee in the Fleet, and the dying words of the latter are, "I hope my merciful Judge will bear in mind

RELIGIOUS SENTIMENTS.   19

trust that laying aside preconceived prejudices, we may set out together in this quest in that spirit of charity and fair inquiry which, at least, is the joint-stock property of all phases of Christianity.

Taking it for granted how strong an advantage an author has, in being free to shape the conditions against as well as for his premises; and taking it for granted that you are willing to lay aside those preconceived prejudices, I shall describe what form I have usually seen them take, and why they are manifestly unfair.

The first comes from those who think that novel-reading and novel-writing are at variance with Christianity, and who repudiate the whole matter upon those grounds.

The second objection comes from those whose reading of these books has been limited to, or has more especially dwelt on, his portraitures of unsavoury and hypocritical professors of religion, and so contend that he always portrayed religious people with either some amount of contempt, or as a sort of harmless, weak-minded class, and that he was especially vicious in delineating the character of parsons, who, they say, are a bad lot, as he has drawn them. Such, in substance, is the charge I have more than once heard fulminated against him.

A third objection is that, in preserving the relevancy of certain characters and supposed narrators, he made religious sentiments to fit them which belong to the characters themselves, and are not his own sentiments.

If there be other grounds of prejudice, I hope to deal with them as my work progresses, but I conceive the above to be the principal, and important enough to deal with in this special place.

Firstly. Without discussing the tendency of novel-reading generally, which forms no part of my plan or engagement, I am content to remark that if Charles Dickens taught Christian truth in *his* novels, he was a

Christian teacher. He never professed to be a theological writer, certainly, but wrote mainly to amuse, and, there is no reason to doubt, thought he was doing a very Christian work by so lightening the burden of this toilsome life for so many who would read what he had written. That much sound religion has been taught through the medium of fiction, and has reached the heart of many who would never have sought elsewhere for it, none who have experience of healthy fiction will care to deny. And none but those who have experience are capable of forming a reliable opinion, and the verdict of those who will impartially form their judgment in such a way cannot possibly be the least affected by the strictures of such a prejudice.

Secondly. The unmasking of hypocrisy is not inconsistent with the character of a Christian teacher and reformer, otherwise Jesus Christ Himself was neither. It would be extremely absurd to infer from the awfully severe strictures of the Saviour upon the time-serving Pharisees, Scribes, and Lawyers that He did not do justice to true religion, and yet something of this sort is in existence with regard to Charles Dickens. Methinks it is the legitimate and dutiful province of all Christian teachers to oppose and show up this worst form of enmity to righteousness in distinct and unfailing terms, and such has Charles Dickens, of all men, done. And had he done only this, without manifesting a regard for genuine Christian character, he would still have rendered a service to religion; but he has done more: he *has* shown a high estimation of true religious character in his books, and has portrayed many unmistakable examples of such.

Let us at once, then, in pursuance of the plan I have projected, examine this matter by the evidence of his own writings. A quotation from his own preface to *The Pickwick Papers* will admirably preface the selections:—

"Lest there be (those) who do not perceive the difference between religion and cant, piety and pretence, a humble reverence for the truths of scripture and an audacious and offensive obtrusion of its letter and not its spirit—let them understand it is always the latter and not the former that is satirised. It is never out of season to protest against that familiarity with sacred things, or against the confounding of Christianity with any class of persons who have just enough religion to make them hate, and not enough to make them love religion."

These remarks are, of course, a vindication of his portraiture of the un-Christian parasite, Stiggins, the representative of a class whom Dickens unrelentingly pursues, throughout his writings, with unsparing reprobation and satire.

We detect varieties of the genus in Chadband, and Brothers Hawkyard and Gimblet, and in Pecksniff, Heep, and a few minor characters. If we admit these are to be found in real life, we will scarcely deny that they are worthy of all the severity with which he treats them. But doubtless there will be many who will object to them as gross caricatures whose attention may be called to a passage in *Martin Chuzzlewit* :—

"Said Dr. Jobling—'Your bosom's lord sits lightly on its throne, Mr. Chuzzlewit, as what's-his-name says in the play. I wish he had said it in a play which did anything but common justice to our profession, by-the-by. There is an apothecary in that drama, sir, which is a low thing ; vulgar, sir ; out of nature altogether.'" (Chapter xli.)

The key-note of that part of the preface to *The Pickwick Papers* quoted is again struck in chapter xlv. of that book, where the character of Stiggins is reckoned up for us in a few sentences, and occasion taken thereby to add a further warning against the cant and pretence of such shallow profession :—

"Mr. Stiggins, getting on his legs as well as he could, proceeded to deliver an edifying discourse for the benefit of the company, but more especially of Mr. Samuel, whom he adjured in moving terms to be upon his guard in that sink of iniquity into which he was cast; to abstain from all hypocrisy and pride of heart; and to take in all things exact pattern and copy by him (Stiggins), in which case he might calculate on arriving, sooner or later, at the comfortable conclusion that, like him, he was a most estimable and blameless character, and that all his acquaintances and friends were hopelessly abandoned and profligate wretches. Which consideration, he said, could not but afford him the liveliest satisfaction.

"He furthermore conjured him to avoid, above all things, the vice of intoxication, which he likened unto the filthy habits of swine, and to those poisonous and baleful drugs which, being chewed in the mouth, are said to filch away the memory. At this point in his discourse the reverend and red-nosed gentleman became singularly incoherent, and staggering to and fro in the excitement of his eloquence, was fain to catch at the back of a chair to preserve his perpendicular.

"Mr. Stiggins did not desire his hearers to be upon their guard against those false prophets and wretched *mockers of religion*, who, without sense to expound its first doctrines, or hearts to feel its first principles, are more dangerous members of society than the common criminal; imposing, as they necessarily do, upon the weakest and worst-informed, casting scorn and contempt upon what *should be most sacred, and bringing into partial disrepute large bodies of virtuous and well-conducted persons of many excellent sects and persuasions.*"

I hope those readers who are apt to take exception at the unsparing criticism of the first two paragraphs of this quotation, and to unjustly aver it to be a sneer at Christianity, have been fair enough to weigh the last paragraph, which it is to be feared they too often do not do in the progress of a hasty and disparaging scanning in quest of material for objection. There they will see that the author distinctly asserts his reverence for Christianity and Christians, and characterises Mr. Stiggins as a mocker of religion. This, too, at a very incipient stage of his experience, when this production may be fairly excused, if excuse be necessary, by the words of the preface to the *Sketches by Boz*, cited at the end of our last chapter.

But, however "crude and ill considered" the character of Stiggins may be, certainly Dickens did not learn, with increasing experience and broader views, to despise the class any the less. Chadband is the conception of maturer years, but in his delineation of it he has seen no reason to reverse his verdict, or to apologise for Stiggins by illuminating Chadband. There is no indecision in the following description :—

"From Mr. Chadband's being much given to describe himself, both verbally and in writing, as a vessel, he is occasionally mistaken by strangers for a gentleman connected with navigation : but he is, as he expresses it, 'in the ministry.' Mr. Chadband is attached to no particular denomination ; and is considered by his persecutors to have nothing so very remarkable to say on the *greatest of subjects* as to render his volunteering, on his own account, at all incumbent on his conscience ; but he had his followers, and Mrs. Snagsby is of the number. . . . Chadband is rather a consuming vessel—the persecutors say a gorging vessel ; and can wield such weapons as a knife and fork remarkably well. . . . Mr. Chadband is a large yellow man, with a fat smile, and a general appearance of having a good deal of train-oil in his system. . . . Mr. Chadband moves softly and cumbrously, not unlike a bear who has been taught to walk upright. He is very much embarrassed about the arms, as if they were inconvenient to him, and he wanted to grovel ; is very much in a perspiration about the head ; and never speaks without first putting up his great hand, as delivering a token to his hearers that he is going to edify them." (*Bleak House*, chapter xix.)

The discourse of Mr. Chadband is in accordance with his character:—

"'My friends,' says he, 'we have partaken in moderation' (which was certainly not the case as far as he was concerned) 'of the comforts which have been provided for us. May this house live upon the fatness of the land; may corn and wine be plentiful therein; may it grow, may it thrive, may it prosper, may it advance, may it proceed, may it press forward! But my friends, have we partaken of anything else? We have. My friends, of what else have we partaken? Of spiritual profit? Yes. From whence have we derived that spiritual profit? My young friend, stand forth!' . . . 'My young friend, you are to us a pearl, you are to us a diamond, you are to us a gem, you are to us a jewel. And why, my young friend?' . . . 'My young friend, it is because you know nothing that you are to us a gem and a jewel. For what are you, my young friend? Are you a beast of the field? No. A bird of the air? No. A fish of the sea or river? No. You are a human boy, my young friend. A human boy. Oh, glorious to be a human boy! And why glorious, my young friend? Because you are capable of receiving the lessons of wisdom, because you are capable of profiting by this discourse which I now deliver for your good, because you are not a stick, or a staff, or a stock, or a stone, or a post, or a pillar.

"'Oh, running stream of sparkling joy,
To be a soaring human boy!'

"'And do you cool yourself in that stream now, my young friend? No. Why do you not cool yourself in that stream now? Because you are in a state of darkness, because you are in a state of obscurity, because you are in a state of sinfulness, because you are in a state of bondage. My young friend, what is bondage? Let us, in a spirit of love, inquire.'" (*Bleak House*, chapter xix.)

This style of discourse the author dubs "abominable nonsense," but assumes that "it must be within everybody's experience, for the Chadband style of oratory is widely received and much admired," and the secret of its composition lies in the "piling of verbose flights of stairs one upon another."

A striking characteristic in Mr. Chadband, and one so oft-repeated and repudiated in other books, that one would suppose the author to take revenge in this way for a once unwilling submission to its baneful influence, is his science in reducing his dealings with heaven to a systematic commercial transaction. In Dickens's own words:—

"It is Mr. Chadband's habit—it is the head and front of his pretensions, indeed—to keep this sort of debtor and creditor account in the smallest items, and to post it publicly on the most trivial occasions." (*Bleak House*, chapter xix.)

On being informed by Guster that the cabman "insists on one-and-eightpence, or on summonizzing the parties," and when Mrs. Snagsby and Mrs. Chadband are proceeding to grow shrill in indignation, Mr. Chadband quiets the tumult by lifting up his hand, and saying:—

"My friends, I remember a duty unfulfilled yesterday. It is right that I should be chastened in some penalty. I ought not to murmur. Rachel, pay the eightpence." (Chapter xix.)

Similarly, when Jo, seeming to have been gradually going out of his mind under the pressure of the reverend gentleman's discourse, gives a terrible yawn, he folds his persecuted chin into its fat smile, looks round, and says:—

"My friend, it is right that I should be humbled, it is right that I should be tried, it is right that I should be mortified, it is right that I should be corrected. I stumbled on Sabbath last, when I thought with pride of my three hours' improving. The account is now favourably balanced, my creditor has accepted a composition. O let us be joyful, joyful! O let us be joyful!" (Chapter xix.)

These sentiments might be left to speak for themselves in

evidence of the author's estimate of such irreligious religion. Their association with the character in whose mouth they are placed renders any explanatory comment unnecessary. But it is forthcoming, if needed, and may be found at the beginning of chapter xliii. of *Nicholas Nickleby*, and is as follows:—

"There are some men who, living with the one object of enriching themselves, no matter by what means, and being perfectly conscious of the baseness and rascality of the means which they will use every day towards this end, affect, nevertheless—even to themselves—a high tone of moral rectitude, and shake their heads and sigh over the depravity of the world. Some of the craftiest scoundrels that ever walked this earth, or rather—for walking implies, at least, an erect position, and the bearing of a man—that ever crawled and crept through life by its dirtiest and narrowest ways, will gravely jot down in diaries the events of every day, and keep a regular debtor and creditor account with Heaven, which shall always show a floating balance in their own favour. Whether this is a gratuitous (the only gratuitous) part of the falsehood and trickery of such men's lives, or whether they really hope to cheat Heaven itself, and lay up treasure in the next world by the same process which has enabled them to lay up treasure in this—not to question how it is, so it is."

Such a man is impersonated in Pecksniff, and such another opportunity is taken to obtrude this hypocritical tendency in his interview with Miss Pinch at the brass and copper-founder's. His introduction of himself is thus commented on:—

"The good man emphasised these words as though he would have said, 'You see in me, young person, the benefactor of your race; the patron of your house; the preserver of your brother, who is fed with manna daily from my table; and in right of whom there is a considerable balance in my favour at present standing in the books beyond the sky.'" (*Martin Chuzzlewit*, chapter ix.)

Again, Mrs. Clennam

"Was always balancing her bargain with the majesty of Heaven, posting up the entries to her credit, strictly keeping her set-off, and claiming her due. She was only remarkable in this, for the force and emphasis with which she did it. Thousands upon thousands do it, according to their varying manner, every day." (*Little Dorrit*, chapter v.)

One more example of the varieties of the Stiggins-Chadband school—Brother Hawkyard, already alluded to—will clear the way for the proposal I made earlier in this chapter, and which I shall fulfil in my next—namely, to show that Dickens had a high regard for true Christian character, and has portrayed many unmistakable Christians, lay and clerical, which will be found to be admirable foils to these, and mark an emphatic contrast.

Brother Hawkyard is introduced as the patron of the orphaned outcast, George Silverman. He is by trade a drysalter, and by choice the popular expounder in a certain religious assembly. The little tale in which he forms a prominent figure was probably composed expressly to emphatically mark, by reiteration as well as description, his unqualified distaste for such professors and such doctrine as Stiggins and Chadband are earlier specimens of. And that his views may be avowed to be all the more emphatic and unalterable, he prefaces his account of Brother Hawkyard's meeting by the following notable words : —

"Let whosoever may peruse these lines kindly take the pains here to read twice my solemn pledge, that what I write here of the language and customs of the congregation in question I write scrupulously, literally, exactly, from the life and the truth.' (George Silverman's explanation, chapter vi.)

Then follows the description, which I quote verbatim :—

"On the first Sunday after I had won what I had so long

tried for, and when it was certain that I was going up to college, Brother Hawkyard concluded a long exhortation thus:—

"'Well, my friends and fellow-sinners, now I told you when I began that I didn't know a word of what I was going to say to you (and no, I did not!); but that was all one to me, because I knew the Lord would put into my mouth the words I wanted.'

("'That's it!' from Brother Gimblet.)

"'And he did put into my mouth the words I wanted.'

("'So he did!' from Brother Gimblet.)

"'And why?'

("'Ah, let's have that!' from Brother Gimblet.)

"'Because I've been his faithful servant for five-and-thirty years, and because He knows it. For five-and-thirty years! And He knows it, mind you! I got those words I wanted on account of my wages. I got 'em from the Lord, my fellow-sinners. Down! I said, Here's a heap of wages due; let us have something down on account. And I got it down, and I paid it over to you; and you won't wrap it up in a napkin, nor yet in a towel, nor yet pocket-handkercher, but you'll put it out at good interest. Very well. Now my brothers and sisters, and fellow-sinners, I am going to commence with a question, and I'll make it so plain (with the help of the Lord, after five-and-thirty years, I should rather hope!) as the devil shall not be able to confuse it in your heads—which he would be overjoyed to do.'

("'Just his way, crafty old blackguard!' from Brother Gimblet.')

"'And the question is this, Are the angels learned?'

("'Not they, not a bit on it!' from Brother Gimblet, with the greatest confidence.)

"'Not they. And where's the proof? Sent ready-made by the hand of the Lord. Why, there's one among us here now, that has got all the learning that could be crammed into him. *I* got him all the learning that could be crammed into him. His grandfather was a brother of ours. He was Brother Parksop. That's what he was. Parksop. Brother Parksop. His worldly name was Parksop, and he was a brother of this brotherhood. Then wasn't he Brother Parksop?'

("'Must be; couldn't help hisself!' from Brother Gimblet.)

"'Well, he left that one here present among us to the care of a brother-sinner of his (and that brother-sinner, mind you, was a sinner of a bigger size in his time than any of you; praise the Lord!) Brother Hawkyard. Me. *I* got him, without fee or reward—without a morsel of myrrh or frankincense, nor yet amber, letting alone the honeycomb—all the learning that could be crammed into him. Has it brought him into our temple in the spirit? No. Have we had any ignorant brothers and sisters in the spirit that didn't know round O from crooked S come in among us meanwhile? Many. Then the angels are *not* learned; then they don't so much as know their alphabet. And now, my friends and fellow-sinners, having brought it to that, perhaps some brother present—perhaps you, Brother Gimblet—will pray a bit for us?'"

So much for Brother Hawkyard's sermon, and four pages further on is a specimen of Brother Hawkyard's prayer, which is chiefly remarkable for the echo it contains of animosity to the Church of England, with the leading doctrines of which body, we are told by the biographer of Charles Dickens, he ever had the strongest sympathy, and, as time went on, found himself able to accommodate all minor differences to. Not that I advance that as an argument for my premises, for I am pledged to make out my case from the writings of the author, and not from the opinions of others, in pursuance of which I call attention to his strictures on congregations of which Brother Hawkyard's is the delineation :—

"From the first I could not like this familiar knowledge of the ways of the sublime, inscrutable Almighty, on Brother Hawkyard's part. As I grew a little wiser, and still a little wiser, I liked it less and less. His manner, too, of confirming himself in a parenthesis—as if, knowing himself, he doubted his own word—I found distasteful. . . . Before the knowledge became forced upon me that outside their place of meeting these brothers and sisters were no better than the rest of the human family, but on the whole were, to put the case mildly, as bad as most, in respect of giving short weight in their shops, and not speaking the truth—I say, before this knowledge became forced upon me, their prolix addresses, their inordinate conceit, their daring ignorance, their investment of the Supreme Ruler of heaven and earth with their own miserable meannesses and littlenesses, greatly shocked me."

That this matter is a sore point with Charles Dickens, and that the sentiments which he puts into the mouth of George Silverman are his own, is apparent from the following paragraph from the *Uncommercial Traveller :—*

"Not that I have any curiosity to hear powerful preachers. Time was, when I was dragged by the hair of my head, as one may say, to hear too many. On summer evenings, when every flower, and tree, and bird might have better addressed my soft young heart, I have in my day been caught in the palm of a female hand by the crown, have been violently scrubbed from the neck to the roots of the hair as a purification for the temple, and have then been carried off highly charged with saponaceous electricity, to be steamed like a potato in the unventilated breath of the powerful Boanerges Boiler and his congregation, until what small mind I had was quite steamed out of me. In which pitiable plight I have been baled out of the place of meeting, at the conclusion of the exercises, and catechised respecting Boanerges Boiler, his fifthly, his sixthly, and his seventhly, until I have regarded that reverend person in the light of a most dismal and oppressive charade. Time was, when I was carried off to platform assemblages at which no human child, whether of wrath or grace, could possibly keep its eyes open, and when I felt the fatal sleep stealing, stealing over me, and when I gradually heard the orator in possession spinning and humming like a great top, until he rolled, collapsed, and tumbled over, and I discovered to my burning shame and fear, that as to that last stage, it was not he, but I. I have sat under Boanerges when he has specially addressed himself to us—us, the infants—and at this present writing I hear his lumbering jocularity (which never amused us, though we basely pretended that it did) and I behold his big round face, and I look up the inside of his outstretched coat-sleeve as if it were a telescope with the stopper on, and I hate him with an unwholesome hatred for two hours." (Chapter ix.)

And all through his life, too, one would imagine, judging from the frequency with which he crops up in his books, in the persons of Stiggins, Chadband, Hawkyard, and minor representatives of the order. We recognise him in the pulpit of Little Bethel (*Old Curiosity Shop*, chapter xli., and no doubt there is a lively recollection of him in the Sunday night school described in *Our Mutual Friend*:—

".... For then, an inclined plane of unfortunate infants would be handed over to the prosiest and worst of all the teachers with good intentions, whom nobody older would endure. Who, taking his stand on the floor before them as chief executioner, would be attended by a conventional volunteer boy as executioner's assistant. When and where it first became the conventional system that a weary or inattentive infant in a class must have its face smoothed downward with a hot hand, or when and where the conventional volunteer boy first beheld such system in operation and became inflamed with a sacred zeal to administer it, matters not. It was the function of the chief executioner to hold forth, and it was the function of the acolyte to dart at sleeping infants, yawning infants, restless infants, whimpering infants, and smooth their wretched faces; sometimes with one hand, as if he were anointing them for a whisker; sometimes with both hands, applied after the fashion of blinkers. And so the jumble would be in action in this department for a mortal hour; the exponent drawling on to My Dearerr Childerenerr, let us say, for example, about the beautiful coming to the sepulchre; and repeating the word sepulchre (commonly used amongst infants) five hundred times, and never once hinting what it meant; the conventional boy smoothing away right and left, as an infallible commentary." (Book ii, chapter i.)

There is a bitter recollection of these days of bondage,

too, in Arthur Clennam's review of the Sundays of his early days :—

"When he sat with his hands before him, scared out of his senses by a horrible tract which commenced business with the poor child by asking him, in its title, why he was going to Perdition?—a piece of curiosity that he in a frock and drawers was really not in a condition to satisfy—and which, for the further attraction of his infant mind, had a parenthesis in every other line with some such hiccuping reference as 2 Ep., Thess. c. iii., v. 6 and 7."

The theme of Arthur Clennam's mother, as a minute and curious study of perverted religion, might be advantageously pursued here, but that she does not fall under the denomination of "hypocrite," which class I am now dealing with. Reserving her, therefore, to a further opportunity, one more companion picture may be added to the foregoing, this time from *David Copperfield:*—

"I well remember the tremendous visages with which we used to go to church, and the changed air of the place. Again the dreaded Sunday comes round, and I file into the old pew first, like a guarded captive brought to a condemned service. Again, Miss Murdstone, in a black velvet gown, that looks as if it had been made out of a pall, follows close upon me ; then my mother ; then her husband. Again, I listen to Miss Murdstone mumbling the responses, and emphasising all the dread words with a cruel relish. Again, I see her dark eyes roll round the church when she says 'miserable sinner,' as if she were calling the congregation names. Again, I wonder with a sudden fear whether it is likely that our good old clergyman can be wrong, and Mr. and Miss Murdstone right, and that all the angels in heaven can be destroying angels? Again, if I move a finger or relax a muscle of my face, Miss Murdstone pokes me with her prayer-book, and makes my side ache." (Chapter iv.)

Small wonder, if such reminiscences as these rankled, as matters of fact, in the memory of the writer, that he should deprecate that "old Puritan spirit," which, he says, "has not tended to make the people less hard in their bargains, or more equal in their dealings"—a sentiment which chimes in with that expressed concerning Brother Hawkyard's congregation.

"Indeed, I am accustomed," he continues, "with reference to great professions and severe faces, to judge of the goods of the other world pretty much as I judge of the goods of this; and whenever I see a dealer in such commodities with too great a display of them in his window, I doubt the quality of the article within." (*American Notes*, chapter v.)

A further quotation from the *American Notes* will clinch the matter for us, and afford us a further insight into his actual religious sentiments than any yet adduced. It is one suggested by his visit to the Perkins Institution and Massachusetts Asylum for the blind at Boston, and is as follows:—

"Ye who have eyes and see not, and have ears and hear not; ye who are the hypocrites of sad countenances, and disfigure your faces that ye may seem unto men to fast; learn healthy cheerfulness and mild contentment from the deaf, and dumb, and blind! Self-elected saints with gloomy brows, this sightless, earless, voiceless child (*i.e.*, Laura Bridgman) may teach you lessons you will do well to follow. Let that poor hand of hers lie gently upon your hearts; for there may be something in its healing touch akin to that of the Great Master whose precepts you misconstrue; whose lessons ye pervert; of whose charity and sympathy with all the world, not one among you in his daily practice knows as much as many of the worst among those fallen sinners, to whom you are liberal in nothing but the preachment of perdition!" (Chapter iii.)

We cannot end our muster-roll of the hypocrites of Dickens without adding to it Sir Edward Chester and Uriah Heep.

The first of these he makes to betray himself, in his own

words and actions, as all hypocrites must do, and the very virtues which he is made to brag of become filthy and vicious in his mouth. Whether he deludes and fascinates Mrs. Varden by his high-sounding submissions to morality, truth, candour, and affection, and adjures himself and her to be sincere—"and Protestant above all things" (in deference to her suggestion), while all the while he is working out a villainous plot; or whether, in the crowning stroke of the same plot, he insinuates the subtle poison of jealousy, concealed in words of honey, into the heart of Miss Haredale, and then avows his machinations to Haredale, with the same *degagé* air and imperturbable self-possession, or whether he skilfully reverses the moral relations between his son and himself, and adopts the shallow lie to break all natural relations with him; or whether he dismisses the beggar with a fervent blessing, "which is as easy as cursing," he said, "and more becoming to the face;" or whether, in the agony of death, he gazes at his murderer with scorn and hatred in his look; but, seeming to remember, even then, that this expression would distort his features after death, he tries to smile—he is a finished picture of the most consummate hyprocrite who ever bedaubed and befouled the robe of moral profession. Religion is not a word to use in association with such a villain, although the master-hand has given us the key-note to what he and such as he profess under that name, in one single sentence put into his mouth:—

". . . Independently of the religious differences between us —and, damn it, that's important." (*Barnaby Rudge*, chapter xii.)

Uriah Heep is a most abominable hypocrite, it is true. His "comfortable convictions" in prison, when, as he says, he "sees his follies," and it is to be added, the inutility of seeing anything more advantageous for his own self-interest, and falls back upon the old trick of "humility, shrewdly blended with religious cant," shows him to be a wily and wary hypocrite and impostor. I cannot refrain from reproducing part of the conversation, which is written in Dickens's best style, and tells so much in so few words:—

"'I would umbly ask, sir, for leave to write again to mother.'
"'It shall certainly be granted,' said Mr. Creakle.
"'Thank you, sir. I am anxious about mother. I am afraid she aint safe.'
"Somebody incautiously asked, What from? But there was a scandalised whisper of 'Hush!'
"'Immortally safe, sir,' returned Uriah, writhing in the direction of the voice. 'I should wish mother to be got into my state. I never should have got into my present state if I hadn't come here. I wish mother had come here. It would be better for everybody if they got took up, and was brought here.'
"This sentiment gave unbounded satisfaction—greater satisfaction, I think, than anything that had passed yet.
"'Before I come here,' said Uriah, stealing a look at us, as if he would have blighted the outer world to which we belonged, if he could, 'I was given to follies; but now I am sensible of my follies. There's a deal of sin outside. There's a deal of sin in mother. There's nothing but sin everywhere—except here.'
"'You are quite changed,' said Mr. Creakle.
"'Oh, dear, yes, sir!' cried this hopeful penitent.
"'You wouldn't relapse if you were going out?' asked somebody else.
"'Oh, de-ar, no, sir!'" (*David Copperfield*, chapter lxi.)

But though Uriah Heep is so detestable a hypocrite, there is more to be said in extenuation for him than there is for Sir John Chester; and Dickens says it, or rather, he makes Uriah say it for himself, and adds such comment as plainly shows that here, as in many other places, he makes his very worst specimens of humanity the pleaders of their own extenuating circumstances, and thus declares his own sentiments. Uriah speaks thus to David Copperfield:—

"'How little you think of the rightful umbleness of a person in my station, Master Copperfield! Father and me was both brought up at a foundation school for boys; and mother, she was likewise brought up at a public sort of charitable establishment. They taught us all a deal of umbleness—not much else that I know of, from morning till night. We was to be umble to this person, and umble to that; and to pull off our caps here, and to make bows there; and always to know our place, and abase ourselves before our betters. And we had such a lot of betters! Father got the monitor-medal by being umble. So did I. Father got made sexton by being umble. He had the character, among the gentle folks, of being such a well-behaved man, that they were determined to bring him in. Be umble, Uriah, says father to me, and you'll get on. It was what was always being dinned into you and me at school; its what goes down best. Be umble, says father, and you'll do. And really it ain't done bad!'

"It was the first time it had ever occurred to me that this detestable cant of false humility might have originated *out* of the Heep family. I had seen the harvest, but had never thought of the seed.

"'When I was quite a young boy,' said Uriah, 'I got to know what umbleness did, and I took to it. I ate umble pie with an appetite. I stopped at the umble part of my learning, and says I, hold hard! When you offered to teach me Latin, I knew better. People like to be above you, says father, keep yourself down. I am very umble to the present moment, Master Copperfield, but I've got a little power.'

"And he said all this—I knew, as I saw his face in the moonlight—that I might understand he was resolved to recompense himself by using his power. I had never doubted his meaning, his craft, and his malice; but I fully comprehended now, for the first time, what a base, unrelenting, and revengeful spirit must have been engendered by this early, and this long, suppression." (Chapter xxxix.)

This partly answers, too, the third objection I proposed to deal with—viz., that in preserving the relevancy of certain characters and supposed narrators, he made religious sentiments to fit them which belong to the characters, and which are not his own personal convictions. Before proceeding to present a contrast to this chapter of hypocrites, I would remark that there are always sufficiently distinctive marks to identify religious and irreligious persons in his writings, and that to preserve this identity, especially in the extreme case of hypocrites and of pronounced Christians, needs something more than a mere superficial spiritual knowledge. Hypocrites, unfortunately, are often well posted up in conventional religious sentiment, and impose upon their credulous admirers, even as Hawkyard, Stiggins, Chadband, Chester, Pecksniff, and Heep are shown to do, and what may be a true piety in the mouths of spiritually enlightened people degenerates into cant in theirs. There is a very different meaning in the "God bless you" of Sir John Chester, and the same benediction uttered by Little Nell, or her good friend the schoolmaster, or by Arthur Clennam or Joe Willet. Mr. Carker says, "Heaven forbid," when the suspicion of his widening the breach between Mr. and Mrs. Dombey appears to be a contingency to be thought of by the latter; and the Single Gentleman, on coming to the village which ends the earthly wanderings of Nell, says, "Pray God we are not too late." The Misses Pecksniff say, "Thank Heaven for this," when their Pa informs them that he and old Anthony Chuzzlewit are reconciled; and Lucie Darnay, receiving her husband from the jaws of the guillotine, exclaims, "Let me thank God for this on my knees." Jonas Chuzzlewit quotes the Bible after a fashion, and of him it is written—

"Is anyone surprised at Mr. Jonas making such a reference to such a book for such a purpose? Does any one doubt the old saw, that the devil (being a layman) quotes Scripture for his own ends?" (*Martin Chuzzlewit*, chapter xi.)

It is noteworthy that those characters whom Dickens

invested with Christian attributes are in the habit of quoting Scripture, and that so appropriately, and with so clear an apprehension of its fullest meaning, that only one conclusion can be drawn therefrom—that in reconciling the person and the sentiment, so as to truly pourtray the character of unaffected Christianity, he displayed that confidence in and experimental apprehension of his subject, by which alone he could have preserved the congruity and truthfulness to reality by which those who are enlightened can only receive it as a coherent and faithful picture.

His very faithfulness in preserving this congruity has laid him open, however, to misrepresentation from stupid and malicious critics, who have pounced upon the sentiments which he put into the mouths of certain characters, and superciliously held them up to the world as his own. Dickens has himself left one notable record of this in a later edition of *Martin Chuzzlewit*, where, in the interview with Jonas Chuzzlewit regarding the marriage settlement, Mr. Pecksniff says:—

"It would sadly pinch and cramp me, my dear friend, but Providence,* perhaps I may be permitted to say a special Providence, has blessed my endeavours, and I could guarantee to make the sacrifice."

In a spirit of exquisite raillery the author continues:—

"A question of philosophy arises here, whether Mr. Pecksniff had or had not good reason to say that he was specially patronised and encouraged in his undertakings. All his life long he had been walking up and down the narrow ways and bye-places, with a hook in one hand and a crook in the other, scraping all sorts of valuable odds and ends into his pouch. Now, there being a special Providence in the fall of a sparrow, it follows (so Mr. Pecksniff would have reasoned) that there must also be a special Providence in the alighting of the stone, or

---

* "That absurd and irreverent conventional phrase." (*Our Mutual Friend*, book i., chapter xi.)

stick, or other substance which is aimed at the sparrow. And Mr. Pecksniff's hook, or crook, having invariably knocked the sparrow on the head and brought him down, that gentleman may have been led to consider himself as specially licensed to bag sparrows, and as being specially seised and possessed of all the birds he had got together. That many undertakings, national as well as individual—but especially the former—are held to be specially brought to a glorious and successful issue, which never could be so regarded on any other process of reasoning, must be clear to all men. Therefore the precedents would seem to show that Mr. Pecksniff had good argument for what he said, and might be permitted to say it, and did not say it presumptuously, vainly, or arrogantly, but in a spirit of high faith and great wisdom, meriting all praise." (Chapter xx.)

. . . .

"The most credulous reader will scarcely believe that Mr. Pecksniff's reasoning was once set upon as the Author's." (*Vide* foot-note on same page.)

It is greatly to be deplored that so great a proportion of the reading public are guilty of the bad practice of devouring books. The average novel-reader is the victim of a morbid and rapacious appetite, which can only be appeased by a rapid succession of startling events and denouements, to gloat over which, every intermediate link is slurred over. To read the novels of Charles Dickens in this unthoughtful spirit is to carry away the falsest of impressions, and to do the greatest of injustice to his genius, for in these points and links of his stories lie some of the very finest touches of his art. The process of development is carried on so uniformly throughout, that every paragraph is necessary to complete the harmony. No wonder, then, that such superficial readers fail to appreciate his writings, which were intended for thoughtful minds, and whose chief merit lies, not so much in inventing startling and tragic situations, as in reasoning them out, and logically showing how great crises in life are led up to by almost imperceptible steps, just as much ignored in real life as in reading novels which, like Dickens's, are true to the life. To lay bare the subtle springs of human action, and to expose those insidious influences which corrupt them, is work worthy of religious and educative recognition, and entitle the writings of Charles Dickens to take their place amongst the reforming agencies in these closely allied principles.

Dickens has said, in one place, that only God knows how a man can impose upon himself. Human experience bears this out very unmistakably; and yet human beings, with all their experience, continue blind to their own frailties, and while they are for ever taking the mote out of the eye of another, wilfully refuse to see the beam which is in their own. The beam is often plainly manifest, but politeness, and interest, and dependency, and many other reasons, incline their associates to tolerate it rather than incur their displeasure by pointing it out. The Word of God threshes out these things unequivocally, but, unhappily, men do not recognise themselves in the portraits delineated therein, notwithstanding their scrupulous fidelity. They see but apostate Jews, and godless Gentiles, and faithless disciples of a past age; they hear warnings and judgments threatened against ancient generations; they marvel at the hypocrisies of the Scribes and Pharisees, but overlook the tremendous fact that under their robes and phylacteries breathed the same nature which exists beneath the coat and trousers of the nineteenth century. To drive home this truth, in modern garments, and with modern surroundings; to show men themselves, actuated by the mean and hypocritical motives which they either have resolutely blinded themselves to the existence of, or else fondly imagine they are successfully concealing from the world, is to go over the same ground that the Bible has covered, and to repeat the same truths in a manner more comprehensible to this generation. And Charles Dickens wrote in such a spirit and with such intentions.

Further: hypocrisy, selfishness, oppression, and evil-doing are painted by Dickens in such unloveliness, and are so constantly reprobated and punished; hidden vice is so uncompromisingly unmasked; youth so earnestly warned against the consequences of that rashness and thoughtless precipitancy to which they are so prone; injustice of every kind so vehemently protested against, and the cause of the weakest and poorest so energetically championed—that we may feel justified in emphasising the desirability of encouraging the circulation of his writings wherever wholesome and educative reading is a *sine quâ non*, and where the object sought thereby is the formation of good character, the cultivation of virtue, and the destruction of innate viciousness.

CHAPTER III.

Dickens a true friend to approved Christian profession.

N replying to the second objection mooted I said that Charles Dickens had not only done Christianity the good service of exposing and lashing hypocrisy, but that he had further shown a high estimation of true religious character, and had pourtrayed many unmistakable examples of such. Be it my task now to mark the antithesis to the unsavoury professors reviewed in the preceding chapter, and to show, from his writings, that he was a true friend to approved Christian profession.

It is idle to say that Dickens habitually spoke slightingly of parsons. Those who say so avow their incapability of judging by virtually admitting their small acquaintance with his writings. Those who are better acquainted with them will agree that the evidence is to the contrary, and will readily recall many parsons in his books who are types of true Christianity, and who are commended as such.

Passing over the Model Curate of "Our Parish," in the *Sketches by Boz*, which is a mere inoffensive character sketch, written at that period for which he claims tolerance for his crudeness and inexperience, we note the clergyman of Dingley Dell, with his "good-humoured, benevolent face

(*Pickwick*, chapter vi.), who was made happy by the happy faces which surrounded the table," and who, after modestly pleading the limitations and homeliness of his sphere of action, in reply to Mr. Pickwick's desire to hear some incident of his experience as a minister of the gospel, relates the story of the " Convict's Return," from which some quotations have been made already. We meet the same clergyman again, if I am not mistaken, in the *Old Curiosity Shop* :—

"He was a simple-hearted old gentleman, of a shrinking, subdued spirit, accustomed to retirement, and very little acquainted with the world, which he had left many years before to come and settle in that place. His wife had died in the house in which he still lived, and he had long since lost sight of any earthly cares or hopes beyond it." (Chapter liii.)

"Good clergymen" are often incidentally mentioned— there is one who marries Arthur Clennam to Little Dorrit, for example—but let us pause awhile to consider the Rev. Frank Milvey, whom we may almost call the model curate of his matured experience, and of whom, in *Our Mutual Friend*, there is a good deal of diffuse information, all very much to his credit, and of which the following are good samples :—

"Reverend Frank Milvey's abode was a very modest abode, because his income was a very modest income. He was officially accessible to every blundering old woman who had incoherence to bestow upon him. . . . He was quite a young man, expensively educated and wretchedly paid, with quite a young wife and half-a-dozen quite young children. He was under the necessity of teaching and translating from the classics to eke out his scanty means, yet was generally expected to have more time to spare than the idlest person in the parish, and more money than the richest. He accepted the needless inequalities and inconsistencies of his life, with a kind of conventional submission that was quite slavish; and any daring layman who would have adjusted such burdens as his would have had small help from him. . . . With a ready patient smile and manner . . . he listened to Mrs. Boffin's statement. (Book i., chapter ix.)

". . . Mrs. Milvey came down. A pretty, bright little woman, something worn by anxiety, who had repressed many pretty tastes and bright fancies, and substituted in their stead, schools, soup, flannel, coals, and all the week-day cares and Sunday coughs of a large population, young and old. As gallantly had Mr. Milvey repressed much in himself that naturally belonged to his old studies and old fellow-students, and taken up among the poor and their children with the hard crumbs of life." (*Ibid.*)

". . . The kind, conscientious couple . . ." (*Ibid.*)

"Then Mr. Boffin took the liberty of mentioning to Mr. Milvey that if Mr. Milvey would do him the favour to be perpetually his banker to the extent of a twenty pound note or so, to be expended without any reference to him, he would be heartily obliged. At this, both Mr. Milvey and Mrs. Milvey were quite as much pleased as if they had no wants of their own, but only knew what poverty was in the persons of other people ; and so the interview terminated with satisfaction and good opinion on all sides." (*Ibid.*)

"The Reverend Frank Milvey, comforting Sloppy, expounded to him how the best of us were more or less remiss in our turning at our respective Mangles—some of us very much so—and how we were all a halting, failing, feeble, and inconstant crew. . . . Sloppy removed his dejected head from the church door, and took it back to the grave in the corner and laid it down there, and wept alone. 'Not a very poor grave,' said the Reverend Frank Milvey, brushing his hand across his eyes, 'when it has that homely figure on it. Richer, I think, than it could be made by most of the sculpture in Westminster Abbey.'" (Book iii., chapter ix.)

"The worthy couple were delayed by a portentous old parishioner of the female gender, who was one of the plagues of their lives, and whom they bore with most exemplary sweetness and good humour. . . . Her most inconvenient characteristic took the form of an impression, usually recurring in inclement weather and about daybreak, that she had something on her mind and stood in immediate need of the Reverend Frank to come and take it off. Many a time had that kind creature got up, and gone out to Mrs. Sprodgkin (such was the disciple's name), suppressing a strong sense of her comicality by his strong sense of duty, and perfectly knowing that nothing but a cold would come of it. However, beyond themselves, the Reverend Frank Milvey and Mrs. Milvey seldom hinted that Mrs. Sprodgkin was hardly worth the trouble she gave; but both made the best of her, as they did of all their troubles." (Book iv., chapter xi.)

The narrative proceeds to tell how, when the worthy couple were in a hurry, both to get to the railway station and to avoid Mrs. Sprodgkin, that that troublesome person was announced, and desired counsel on a trivial matter. She was bought off, on this occasion, by a present of tea, etc., but persisted on dutifully remaining in the hall to curtsey to the Reverend Frank, which involved him in a discursive address, and caused him at length to hurry, with Mrs. Milvey, in a heated condition to the railway station.

"All of which is here recorded to the honour of that *good Christian pair, representatives of hundreds of other good Christian pairs, as conscientious and as useful,* who merge the smallness of their work in its greatness, and feel in no danger of losing dignity when they adapt themselves to incomprehensible humbugs."

"'Detained at the last moment by one who had a claim upon me,' was the Reverend Frank's apology to Lightwood, taking no thought to himself." (*Ibid.*)

Turning now to the *American Notes*, we may read how Dickens—

"Was reluctantly obliged to forego the delight of hearing Dr. Channing, who happened to preach that morning for the first time in a very long interval. I mention the name of this distinguished and accomplished man (with whom I soon afterwards had the pleasure of becoming personally acquainted), that

I may have the gratification of recording my humble tribute of admiration and respect for his high abilities and character; and for the bold philanthropy with which he ever opposed himself to that most hideous blot and foul disgrace—slavery." (Chapter iii.)

To this literal record of his personal sentiments, written in a book of his own experiences, may be added a remark which follows immediately upon the reminiscences of Boanerges Boiler:—

"Now, I have heard many preachers since that time—not powerful; merely Christian, unaffected, and reverential—and I have many such preachers on my roll of friends." (*Uncommercial Traveller*, chapter ix.)

If there are those whose susceptibilities have been irritated by the recorded utterances of Messrs. Stiggins, Chadband, and Hawkyard, and the fun made of their empty cant, they will surely be reconciled when two records of real Christian preachers are adduced, with their sermons to boot, from the last two quoted books.

In the *American Notes*, after remarking that the peculiar province of the Pulpit in New England (always excepting the Unitarian ministry) would appear to be the denouncement of all innocent and rational amusements, and that those ministers who strew the Eternal Path with the greatest amount of brimstone, and who enlarge with the greatest pertinacity on the difficulty of getting into heaven, are most popular, he proceeds to say:—

"The only preacher I heard in Boston was Mr. Taylor, who addresses himself peculiarly to seamen, and who was once a mariner himself. I found his chapel down among the shipping, in one of the narrow, old, water-side streets, with a gay, blue flag waving freely from its roof. In the gallery opposite to the pulpit were a little choir of male and female singers, a violoncello, and a violin. The preacher already sat in the pulpit, which was raised on pillars, and ornamented behind him with painted drapery of a lively and somewhat theatrical appearance.

He looked a weather-beaten, hard-featured man of about six or eight and fifty ; with deep lines graven as it were into his face, dark hair, and a stern, keen eye. Yet the general appearance of his countenance was pleasant and agreeable. The service commenced with a hymn, to which succeeded an extemporary prayer. It had the fault of frequent repetition, incidental to all such prayers ; but it was plain and comprehensive in its doctrines, and breathed a tone of general sympathy and charity, which is not so commonly a characteristic of this form of address to the Diety as it might be. That done, he opened his discourse, taking for his text a passage from the Song of Solomon, laid upon the desk before the commencement of the service by some unknown member of the congregation :—'Who is this coming up from the wilderness, leaning on the arm of her beloved?'

" He handled his text in all kinds of ways, and twisted it into all manner of shapes ; but always ingeniously, and with a rude eloquence well adapted to the capability of his hearers. Indeed, if I be not mistaken, he studied their sympathies and understandings much more than the display of his own powers. His imagery was all drawn from the sea, and from the incidents of a seaman's life ; and was often remarkably good. He spoke to them of ' that glorious man, Lord Nelson,' and of Collingwood ; and drew nothing in, as the saying is, by the head and shoulders, but brought it to bear upon his purpose, naturally, and with a sharp mind to its effect. Sometimes, when much excited with his subject, he had an odd way—compounded of John Bunyan and Balfour of Burley—of taking his great quarto Bible under his arm, and pacing up and down the pulpit with it ; looking steadily down, meantime, into the midst of the congregation. Thus, when he applied his text to the first assemblage of his hearers, and pictured the wonder of the church at their presumption in forming a congregation amongst themselves, he stopped short with his Bible under his arm in the manner I have described, and pursued his discourse after this manner :—

"'Who are these—who are they—who are these fellows ? Where do they come from ? Where are they going to ? Come from ! What's the answer ?'—leaning out of the pulpit, and pointing downward with his right hand : ' From below !'— starting back again, and looking at the sailors before him

'From below, my brethren. From under the hatches of sin, battened down above you by the evil one. That's where you came from!'—a walk up and down the pulpit : 'And where are you going?'—stopping abruptly : 'Where are you going? Aloft!'—very softly, and pointing upwards : 'Aloft!'—louder : 'Aloft!'—louder still : 'That's where you are going—with a fair wind—all taut and trim, steering direct for heaven in its glory, where there are no storms or foul weather, and where the wicked cease from troubling and the weary are at rest.'— Another walk : 'That's where you're going to, my friends. That's it. That's the place. That's the port. That's the haven. It's a blessed harbour—still water there, in all changes of the winds and tides ; no driving ashore upon the rocks, or slipping your cables and running out to sea, there : Peace— Peace—Peace—all peace!'—Another walk, and patting the Bible under his left arm : 'What! These fellows are coming from the wilderness, are they? Yes. From the dreary, blighted Wilderness of Iniquity, whose only crop is Death. But do they lean upon anything—do they lean upon nothing, these poor seamen?'—Three raps upon the Bible : 'Oh, yes.— Yes.—They lean upon the arm of their Beloved'—three more, and a walk : 'Pilot, guiding-star, and compass, all in one, to all hands—here it is'—three more : 'Here it is. They can do their seaman's duty manfully, and be easy in their minds in the utmost peril and danger, with this'—two more : 'They can come, even these poor fellows can come, from the wilderness, leaning on the arm of their Beloved, and go up—up—up!' —raising his hand higher and higher, at every repetition of the word, so that he stood with it at last stretched above his head, regarding them in a strange, rapt manner, and pressing the book triumphantly to his breast, until he gradually subsided into some other portion of his discourse.

"I have cited this, rather as an instance of the preacher's eccentricities than his merits, though, taken in connection with his look and manner, and the character of his audience, even this was striking. It is possible, however, that my favourable impression of him may have been greatly influenced and strengthened—firstly, by his impressing upon his hearers that the true observance of religion was not inconsistent with a cheerful deportment and an exact discharge of the duties of their station, which, indeed, it scrupulously required of them; and secondly, by his cautioning them not to set up any monopoly in Paradise and its mercies. I never heard these two points so wisely touched (if, indeed, I have ever heard them touched at all) by any preacher of that kind before." (*American Notes*, chapter iii.)

In the *Uncommercial Traveller* he records the particulars of two journeys, in that capacity, to a great East End Theatre. The first was made on a Saturday night, to see the play, and the second on the following Sunday night, to hear the preaching. His relation of and remarks on the second affords us a great insight into his religious convictions:—

"A portion of Scripture was being read as I went in. It was followed by a discourse, to which the congregation listened with most exemplary attention and uninterrupted silence and decorum. My own attention comprehended both the auditory and the speaker, and shall turn to both in this recalling of the scene, exactly as it did at the time.

"A very different thing, I thought, when the discourse began, to speak appropriately to so large an audience, and to speak with tact. Without it, better not to speak at all. *Infinitely better to read the New Testament well, and to let that speak.* In this congregation there is indubitably one pulse; but I doubt if any power short of genius can touch it as one, and make it answer as one.

"I could not possibly say to myself, as the discourse proceeded, that the minister was a good speaker. I could not possibly say to myself that he expressed an understanding of the general mind and character of his audience. There was a suppositious working-man introduced into the homily, to make suppositious objections to our Christian religion and be reasoned down, who was not only a very disagreeable person, but remarkably unlike life—very much more unlike it than anything I had seen in the pantomime. The native independence of character this artisan was supposed to possess, was represented by a suggestion of a dialect that I certainly never heard in my uncommercial travels, and with a coarse swing of voice and manner anything but agreeable to his feelings I should conceive, considered in the light of a portrait, and as far away from the fact as a Chinese Tartar. There was a model pauper introduced in like manner, who appeared to me to be the most intolerably arrogant pauper ever relieved, and to show himself in absolute want and dire necessity of a course of stone yard. For, how did this pauper testify to his having received the gospel of humility? A gentleman met him in the workhouse, and said (which I really thought very good-natured of him), 'Ah, John? I am sorry to see you here. I am sorry to see you so poor.' 'Poor, sir!' replied the man, drawing himself up, 'I am the son of a prince! My father is the King of kings. My father is the Lord of lords. My father is the Ruler of all the princes of the earth!' etc. And this was what all the preacher's fellow-sinners might come to, if they would embrace this blessed book—which I must say it did some violence to my own feelings of reverence to see held out at arm's length at frequent intervals and soundingly slapped, like a slow lot at a sale. Now, could I help asking myself the question, whether the mechanic before me, who must detect the preacher as being wrong about the visible manner of himself and the like of himself, and about such a noisy lip-server as that pauper, might not, most unhappily for the usefulness of the occasion, doubt that preacher's being right about things not visible to human senses?

"Again. Is it necessary or advisable to address such an audience continually as 'fellow-sinners'? Is it not enough to be fellow-creatures, born yesterday, suffering and striving to-day, dying to-morrow? By our common humanity, my brothers and sisters, by our common capacities for pain and pleasure, by our common laughter and our common tears, by our common aspiration to reach something better than ourselves, by our common tendency to believe in something good, and to invest whatever we love or whatever we lose with some qualities that are superior to our own failings and weaknesses as we know them in our own hearts—by these, Hear me!—Surely it is enough to be fellow-creatures. Surely it includes the other designation, and some touching meanings over and above.

"Again, there was a personage introduced into the discourse (not an absolute novelty, to the best of my remembrance of my reading), who had been personally known to the preacher, and had been quite a Crichton in all the ways of philosophy, but had been an infidel. Many a time had the preacher talked with him on that subject, and many a time had he failed to convince that intelligent man. But he fell ill, and died, and before he died he recorded his conversion in words which the preacher had taken down, my fellow-sinners, and would read to you from this piece of paper. I must confess that to me, as one of an uninstructed audience, they did not appear particularly edifying. I thought their tone exceedingly selfish, and I thought they had a spiritual vanity in them which was of the before-mentioned refractory pauper's family.

"All slangs and twangs are objectionable everywhere, but the slang and twang of the conventicle—as bad in its way as that of the House of Commons, and nothing worse can be said of it—should be studiously avoided under such circumstances as I describe. The avoidance was not complete on this occasion. Nor was it quite agreeable to me to see the preacher addressing his pet 'points' to his backers on the stage, as if appealing to those disciples to show him up, and testify to the multitude that each of those points was a clincher.

"But, in respect of the large Christianity of his general tone; of his renunciation of all priestly authority; of his earnest and reiterated assurance to the people that the commonest among them could work out their own salvation if they would, by simply, lovingly, and dutifully following Our Saviour, and that they needed the mediation of no erring man; in these particulars this gentleman deserved all praise. Nothing could be better than the spirit, or the plain emphatic words of his discourse in these respects; and it was a most significant and encouraging circumstance that whenever he struck that chord, or whenever he described anything which Christ Himself had done, the array of faces before him was very much more earnest, and very much more expressive of emotion, than at any other time. . . . The time appointed for the conclusion of the proceedings was eight o'clock. The address having lasted until full that time, and it being the custom to conclude with a hymn, the preacher intimated in a few sensible words that the clock had struck the hour, and that those who desired to go before the hymn was sung could go now, without giving offence. No one stirred. The hymn was then sung, in good time and tune and unison, and its effect was very striking. A comprehensive benevolent prayer dismissed the throng. . . . "* (Chapter iv.)

But his highest and most unqualified approbation is reserved for a certain clergyman of real life, whose meritorious services in connection with the memorable and terrible wreck of the *Royal Charter,* Australian trader and passenger ship, homeward bound (that struck on the coast of Anglesey on the 26th of October 1859, broke into three parts, went down with her treasure of five hundred human lives, and has never stirred since), he records in the *Uncommercial Traveller.*

It is a marvellously graphic and affecting picture which Charles Dickens has left us of this sad event and its results, and to which is earnestly commended the attention of those who have not hitherto read it. Our present concern with it lies in the relation which the clergyman who is connected with the relation occupies towards it—

"It was the clergyman himself (who is previously mentioned as being amongst the first helpers on the scene of the catastrophe) from whom I heard this, while I stood on the shore, looking in his kind wholesome face as it turned to the spot. . . . It was the kind and wholesome face I have made mention of as being then beside me, that I had purposed to myself to see, when I left home for Wales. I had heard of that clergyman, as having buried many scores of the shipwrecked people; of his having opened his house and heart to their agonised friends; of his having used a most sweet and patient diligence for weeks and weeks, in the performance of the forlornest offices that man can render to his kind; of his having most tenderly and thoroughly devoted himself to the dead, and to those who were sorrowing for the dead. I had said to myself in the Christmas

---

* The further remarks on this service will be quoted in another place.

season of the year, I should like to see that man! And he had swung the gate of his little garden in coming out to meet me not half-an-hour ago.

"So cheerful of spirit and so guiltless of affectation, as true practical Christianity ever is! I read more of the New Testament in the fresh frank face going up the village beside me, in five minutes, than I have read in anathemising discourses (albeit put to press with enormous flourishing of trumpets), in all my life. *I heard more of the Sacred Book in the cordial voice that had nothing to say about its owner*, than in all the would-be celestial pairs of bellows that have ever blown conceit at me.

. . . .

"The cheerful earnestness of this good Christian minister was as consolatory as the circumstances out of which it shone were sad. I have never seen anything more delightfully genuine than the calm dismissal by himself and his household of all they had undergone, as a simple duty* that was quietly done and ended. In speaking of it, they spoke of it with great compassion for the bereaved; but laid no stress upon their own hard share in those weary weeks, except as it had attached many people to them as friends, and elicited many touching expressions of gratitude. This clergyman's brother—himself the clergyman of two adjoining parishes, who had buried thirty-four of the bodies in his own churchyard, and who had done to them all that his brother had done as to the larger number—must be understood as included in the family. He was there, with his neatly-arranged papers, and made no more account of his trouble than anybody else did. Down to yesterday's post outward, my clergyman alone had written one thousand and seventy-five letters to relatives and friends of the lost people. In the absence of self-assertion, it was only through my now and then delicately putting a question as the occasion arose, that I had become informed of these things. It was only when I had remarked again and again, in the church, on the awful nature of the scene of death he had been required so closely to familiarise himself with for the soothing of the living, that he had casually said, without the least abatement of his cheerful-

---

* A perusal of the article from which this is quoted will show how absorbing, painful, and laborious a duty it really was.

ness, 'Indeed, it had rendered him unable for a time to eat or drink more than a little coffee now and then, and a piece of bread.'

"In this noble modesty, in this beautiful simplicity, in this serene avoidance to 'improve' an occasion which might be supposed to have sunk of its own weight into my heart, I seemed to have happily come, in a few steps, from the churchyard, with its open grave, which was the type of Death, to the Christian dwelling side by side with it, which was the type of Resurrection. I shall never think of the former without the latter. The two will always rest side by side in my memory. If I had lost any one dear to me in this unfortunate ship, if I had made a voyage from Australia to look at the grave in the churchyard, I should go away, thankful to God that that house was so close to it, and that its shadow by day and its domestic light by night fell upon the earth in which its master had so tenderly laid my dear one's head."

Here follow copies of some of the numerous letters received by this clergyman from friends and relatives of the victims of the catastrophe, which the author leaves to themselves, to give expression to his own estimation of that good man. Doubtless, having selected those which he considered most remarkable, and best calculated to strengthen his own opinion of him to whom they were addressed, we may reasonably look in them for the echo of his own religious sentiments, in the testimony they bear to the Christianity of the clergyman (as Dickens understood Christianity), as well as their agreement with his own.

The following extracts are striking, as bearing on these views. Others who read them may find remarks which are as conclusive to their minds:—

"My darling . . . was a most amiable and obedient child, early taught the way of salvation."

. . . .

"I . . . do thank you most kindly for the interest you have taken about my dear husband, as well as for the sentiments your letter contains, evincing the spirit of a Christian who can sympathise with those who, like myself, are broken down with grief. . . . Time may roll on and bear its sons away, but your name as a disinterested person will stand in history."

* * * * *

"God grant that your prayers over him may reach the mercy seat, and that his soul may be received (through Christ's intercession) into heaven!"

* * * * *

"I am overpowered when I think of you and your hospitable home. No words could speak language suited to my heart. I refrain. God reward you with the same measure you have meted with!"

* * * * *

"I must again repeat, that language has no words by which I can express my sense of obligation to you. . . . I have seen him! and can now realise my misfortune more than I have hitherto been able to do. Oh, the bitterness of the cup I drink! But I bow submissive. God *must* have done right. I do not want to feel less, but to acquiesce more simply."

* * * * *

From a Jewish congregation—"You have, indeed, like Boaz, not left off your kindness to the living and the dead. You have not alone acted kindly towards the living by receiving them hospitably at your house, and energetically assisting them in their mournful duty, but also towards the dead, *by exerting yourself to have our co-religionists buried in their own ground, and according to our rites.*"

* * * * *

The narrative thus concludes :—

"Convocations, Conferences, Diocesan Epistles, and the like will do a great deal for religion, I dare say, and heaven send they may! but I doubt if they will ever do their Master's service half so well, in all the time they last, as the heavens have seen it done in this bleak spot upon the rugged coast of Wales.

"Had I lost the friend of my life, in the wreck of the *Royal Charter;* had I lost my betrothed, the more than friend of my life; had I lost my maiden daughter, had I lost my hopeful boy, had I lost my little child; I would kiss the hands that worked so busily and gently in the church, and say, 'None better could have touched the form, though it had lain at home!' I could be sure of it, I could be thankful for it. I could be content to leave the grave near the house the good family pass in and out of every day, undisturbed, in the little churchyard where so many are so strangely brought together." (*Uncommercial Traveller*, chapter ii.)

We shall now be able, bearing the evidence of this chapter in mind, not only to make allowances for the strictures upon Stiggins and Company, but to dispassionately investigate those of Dickens's writings in which he speaks of what he condemns and objects to in religious practice, which will reasonably complete this section of our evidence, and open the way for the consideration of his own defined religious views.

CHAPTER IV.

What he condemns and objects to in Religious practice.

"ALL good things perverted to evil purposes," says Gabriel Varden, the locksmith, "are worse than those which are naturally bad. When religion goes wrong, she is very wrong." (*Barnaby Rudge*, chapter li.)

The occasion of Mr. Varden's sentiment is Mrs. Varden's discovery that she has been lending her aid and sympathy to a misdirected and mischievous cause, which, ostensibly professing to maintain true religion, prostituted it to the basest uses.

The remarkable agitation known in history as the "No-Popery Riots of 'Eighty" is graphically delineated in *Barnaby Rudge;* and by skilful management of the characters, and powerful description of events, rather than by comment, the sources and secret springs of the movement are laid open, and a striking picture presented to us of the great evils of religious bigotry and intolerance, in the course of which a great deal of insight may be obtained into the religious sentiments of Charles Dickens.

The two prime movers are Lord George Gordon and his secretary. The former is a curious psychological study. In his indecision and restlessness of purpose, his doubt of himself, and his manner of appealing to Gashford to confirm his wavering faith; in his half-expressed suspicions of the honesty and conscientiousness of his followers, of whom he complains that there were "some plaguey, ill-looking characters amongst them;" in his nervous doubt of the righteousness of even the cause to which he is pledged; in the feverish excitement into which he is lashed by Gashford, and under the influences of which only can he exhibit enthusiasm in it; and in his unsuspicious reception of the grossest and most transparent flattery—he gives sufficient evidence of the author's estimate of the unsound sources of the no-popery riots. Its malicious and evil side is exhibited in the parallel picture of Gashford, who is described as having an overhanging brow, great hands and feet, a pair of eyes that seemed to have made an unnatural retreat into his head, and to have dug a cave to hide in; a manner smooth and humble, but very sly and slinking, like that of a man who was always lying in wait for something that wouldn't come to pass, and he fawned like a spaniel dog. (Chapter xxxv.) In his skilful leading on of his patron; in his abject deference to him as a superior, and his obvious using of him as a despised tool; in the lie which his naturally repulsive and malicious countenance gives to his profession; in the gross adulation he lavishes over Lord George when he pretends to suppose he is asleep—he is the evil genius of the wretched doings, for the excesses of which he is shown to be mainly responsible.

There is a vast and notable difference between the character of these two men, and a painstaking distinction made between the motives by which each is actuated, plainly teaching us that, from the author's point of view, the no-popery movement was a compound of error and malice, of mental weakness and diabolical cunning, of sincere but perverted religious views on the one hand, and of hatred to all religion on the other. Compare the following selections, and we gain a very reasonable insight into the mainsprings and secret workings of this very remarkable movement :—

"Although there was something very ludicrous in his (Lord George Gordon's) vehement manner, taken in conjunction with his meagre aspect and ungraceful presence, it would scarcely have provoked a smile in any man of kindly feeling ; or even if it had, he would have felt sorry and almost angry with himself next moment for yielding to the impulse. *This lord was sincere in his violence and in his wavering.* A nature prone to false enthusiasm, and the vanity of being a leader, were the worst qualities apparent in his composition. All the rest was weakness —sheer weakness ; and it is the unhappy lot of thoroughly weak men, that their very sympathies, affections, confidences—all the qualities which in better constituted minds are virtues—dwindle into foibles, or turn into downright vices." (Chapter xxxvi.)

"Lord George Gordon, remaining in his prison in the Tower of London until the 5th of February in the following year, was on that day solemnly tried at Westminster for high treason. Of this crime he was, after a patient investigation, declared not guilty, upon the ground that there was no proof of his having called the multitude together with any traitorous or unlawful intentions. . . . For seven years afterwards he remained quiet, at the strong intercession of his friends, saving that he, every now and then, took occasion to display his zeal for the Protestant faith in some extravagant proceeding which was the delight of its enemies. . . . In the year 1788 he was stimulated by some new insanity to write and publish an injurious pamphlet, reflecting on the Queen of France. . . . In August 1788 he made a profession of the Jewish religion. . . . Deserted by his former friends, and treated in all respects like the worst criminal in the jail, he lingered on, quite cheerful and resigned, until the 1st of November 1793, when he died in his cell. . . . Many men with fewer sympathies for the distressed and needy, with less abilities and harder hearts, have made a shining figure and left a brilliant fame. He had his mourners. The prisoners bemoaned his loss, and missed him ; for though his means were not large, his charity was great, and in bestowing alms among them he considered the necessities of all alike, and knew no distinction of sect or creed. There are wise men in the highways of the world who may learn something, even from this poor crazy lord in Newgate." (Chapter lxxxii.)

"Gashford, with many a sly look towards the bed, sat chuckling at his master's folly, until his deep and heavy breathing warned him that he might retire." (Chapter xxxvi.)

"'Dreamed he was a Jew,' said Gashford, thoughtfully, as he closed the bedroom door. 'He may come to that before he dies. It's like enough. Well! After a time, and provided I lost nothing by it, I don't see why that religion shouldn't suit me as well as any other. There are rich men among the Jews; shaving is very troublesome;—yes, it would suit me well enough. For the present, though, we must be Christian to the core. Our prophetic motto * will suit all creeds in their turn, that's a comfort.'" (Chapter xxxvii.)

"'The cause!' repeated the secretary, looking at him in a sort of abstraction. 'There is no cause. The cause is lost.'

"'Lost!'

"'Oh yes. You have heard, I suppose?' . . .

"'What would you have us do, master?' cried Hugh.

"'Nothing,' returned Gashford, shrugging his shoulders. 'Nothing. When my lord was reproached and threatened for standing by you, I, as a prudent man, would have had you do nothing. When the soldiers were trampling you under foot, I would have had you do nothing. When one of them was struck down by a daring hand, and I saw confusion and dismay in all their faces, I would have had you do nothing—just what you did, in short . . . If you are cast into prison; if the young man is dragged from us and from his friends; perhaps from people whom he loves, and whom his death would kill; is thrown into jail, brought out and hanged before their eyes; still, do nothing. You'd find it your best policy.'

"'Come on!' cried Hugh, striding toward the door. 'Dennis —Barnaby—come on!'

* "Called, and chosen, and faithful."

"'Where? To do what?' said Gashford, slipping past him, and standing with his back against it.

"'Anywhere! Anything!' cried Hugh. 'Stand aside, master, or the window will serve our turn as well. Let us out!'

"'Ha, ha, ha! You are of such—of such an impetuous nature,' said Gashford, changing his manner for one of the utmost good fellowship and the pleasantest raillery; 'you are such an excitable creature—but you'll drink with me before you go? . . . Some liquor here! Be quick, or he'll not stop, even for that. He is a man of such desperate ardour! Once roused, he is a fellow of such fierce determination. . . . I hear,' he said, smoothly, as he stood among them with a great measure of liquor in his hand, and filled their glasses as quickly and as often as they chose, 'I hear—but I cannot say whether it is true or false—that the men who are loitering in the streets to-night are half disposed to pull down a Romish chapel or two, and that they only want leaders. I even heard mention of those in Duke Street, Lincoln's Inn Fields, and in Warwick Street, Golden Square; but common report, you know—You are not going?'

"——'To do nothing, master, eh?' cried Hugh. 'No jails and halter for Barnaby and me. They must be frightened out of that. Leaders are wanted, are they? Now, boys!'

"'A most impetuous fellow!' cried the secretary. 'Ha, ha! a courageous, boisterous, most vehement fellow! A man who——'

"There was no need to finish the sentence, for they had rushed out of the house, and were far beyond hearing. He stopped in the middle of a laugh, listened, drew on his gloves, and clasping his hands behind him, paced the deserted room for a long time . . . (Chapter i.).

"'I would have you,' said Gashford, pinching his arm with such malevolence that his nails seem to meet in the skin; 'I would have you put some meaning into your work. Fools! Can you make no better bonfires than of rags and scraps? Can you burn nothing whole?'" (Chapter lii.)

"Gashford, crouching yet malignant, raised his scowling face, like Sin subdued, and pleaded to be gently used. 'I have access to all my lord's papers,' he said, in a submissive voice:

'There are many important documents amongst them. There are a great many in secret drawers, and distributed in various places, known only to my lord and me. I can give you some very valuable information, and render important assistance to any inquiry. You will have to answer for it if I receive ill-usage.'" (Chapter lxxi.)

"He subsisted for a time upon his master's secrets; and, this trade failing when the stock was quite exhausted, procured an appointment in the honourable corps of spies and eavesdroppers employed by the Government." (Chapter lxxxi.)

Of the prominent and trusted agents of Gashford, Dennis, the hangman, and Hugh, two extracts will sum up the total of their Protestant faith and zeal:—

"'Well, then, look here,' said the hangman. 'If these Papists get into power, and begins to boil and roast instead of hang, what becomes of my work? If they touch my work, that's a part of so many laws, what becomes of the laws in general, what becomes of the religion, what becomes of the country?— Did you ever go to church, Muster Gashford? . . . I've been once—twice, counting the time I was christened—and when I heard the parliament prayed for, and thought how many new hanging laws they made every session, I considered that *I* was prayed for. Now mind, Muster Gashford, I mustn't have my Protestant work touched, nor this here Protestant state of things altered in no degree, if I can help it; I mustn't have no Papists interfering with me, unless they come to be worked off in course of law; I mustn't have no boiling, no roasting, no frying—nothing but hanging. My lord may well call me an earnest fellow. In support of the great Protestant principle of having plenty of that, I'll burn, fight, kill—do anything you bid me, so that its bold and devilish—though the end of it was, that I got hung myself.—There, Muster Gashford!'

"He appropriately followed up this *frequent prostitution of a noble word* to the vilest purposes, by pouring out in a kind of ecstasy at least a score of tremendous oaths; then wiped his heated face upon his neckerchief, and cried, 'No Popery! I'm a religious man, by G——!'" (Chapter xxxvii.)

"'No Popery, brother!' cried the hangman.

"'No Property, brother!' responded Hugh.

"'Popery, popery,' said the Secretary, with his usual mildness.

"'It's all the same!' cried Dennis. 'It's all right. Down with him, Muster Gashford. Down with everybody! Down with everything! Hurrah for the Protestant religion! That's the time of day, Muster Gashford!'" (*Ibid.*)

The graphic descriptions of the rioters, and the exciting details of their evil and bloodthirsty work, lead the reader to understand how largely impregnated their ranks were with such stuff as Dennis and Hugh. Certainly it is admitted that the throng was doubtless sprinkled here and there with honest zealots, but was composed for the most part of the very scum and refuse of London, whose growth was fostered by bad criminal laws, bad prison regulations, and the worst conceivable police (Vol. ii). The mad excesses and wholesale destruction in which their "Protestant zeal" expended itself, and which is minutely described, is a sufficient index to their motives; and if any religious principle may be described in their behaviour, it must be of a kindred character to that which animated Mrs. Varden, "who was most devout when most ill-tempered," "like some other ladies who in remote ages flourished upon this globe." (Chapter iv.)

" It was a most exquisite satire upon the false religious cry which had led to so much misery, that some of these people" (those of the rioters who were condemned to death for their participation) "owned themselves to be Catholics, and begged to be attended by their own priests." (Chapter lxxvii.)

The following extract will be read with interest, as bearing more directly, and as a matter of personal sentiment, upon the sources and secret of this movement :—

" To surround anything, however monstrous or ridiculous, with an air of mystery, is to invest it with a secret charm, and power of attraction which to the crowd is irresistible. False priests, false prophets, false doctors, false patriots, false prodigies of every kind veiling their proceedings in mystery, have always addressed themselves at an immense advantage to the popular credulity, and have been, perhaps, more indebted to that resource in gaining and keeping for a time the upper hand of Truth and Common Sense, than to any half-dozen items in the whole catalogue of imposture. Curiosity is, and has been from the creation of the world, a master-passion. To awaken it, to gratify it by slight degrees, and yet leave something always in suspense, is to establish the surest hold that can be had, in wrong, on the unthinking part of mankind.

"If a man had stood on London Bridge, calling till he was hoarse upon the passers-by, to join with Lord George Gordon, although for an object which no man understood, and which in that very incident had a charm of its own—the probability is, that he might have influenced a score of persons in a month. If all zealous Protestants had been publicly urged to join an association for the avowed purpose of singing a hymn or two occasionally, and hearing some indifferent speeches made, and ultimately of petitioning Parliament not to pass an act for abolishing the penal laws against Roman Catholic priests, the penalty of perpetual imprisonment denounced against those who educated children in that persuasion, and the disqualification of all members of the Romish Church to inherit real property in the United Kingdom by right of purchase or descent—matters so far removed from the business and bosoms of the mass might, perhaps, have called together a hundred people. But when vague rumours got abroad, that in this Protestant association a secret power was mustering against the Government for undefined and mighty purposes; when the air was filled with whispers of a confederacy among the Popish powers to degrade and enslave England, establish an Inquisition in London, and turn the pens of Smithfield into stakes and cauldrons; when terrors and alarms which no man understood were perpetually broached, both in and out of Parliament, by one enthusiast who did not understand himself, and bygone bugbears, which had lain quietly in their graves for centuries, were raised again to haunt the ignorant and credulous; when all this was done, as it were, in the dark, and secret invitations to join the Great Protestant Association in defence of religion, life, and liberty, were dropped in the public ways, thrust under the house-doors, tossed in at windows, and pressed into the hands of those who trod the streets at night ; when they glared from every wall, and shone on every post and pillar, so that stocks and stones appeared infected with the common fear, urging all men to join together blindfold in resistance of they knew not what, they knew not why—then the mania spread indeed, and the body, still increasing every day, grew 40,000 strong." (Chapter xxxvii.)

Thus emphatically here, as in other places, Charles Dickens earnestly deprecates the curse of fanatical bigotry and misdirected religious zeal. He has none the more sympathy with the no-popery movement, even in its more innocent and honester aspects, because he associates Protestantism with that which is noble, and because "he had never any sympathy so strong as with the leading doctrines of the Church of England." His impartiality is markedly shown in his manner of dealing with this subject. It was a wrong and a mischievous movement, without a redeeming feature ; and he does not attempt to introduce the element of "right" into that which was wrong altogether, not even to palliate it because it was a protest against Romanism, with which creed he declares plainly, in the preface to *Barnaby Rudge*, that he has no sympathy. I hasten to quote it, to complete the record of his sentiments on the no-popery riots, and to preface his views on the subject just alluded to, which, in fairness, and for completeness of my work, I feel bound to do :—

" It is unnecessary to say, that those shameful tumults, while they reflect indelible disgrace upon the time in which they occurred, and all who had act or part in them, teach a good lesson. That what we falsely call a religious cry is easily raised by men who have no religion, and who in their daily practice set at naught the commonest principles of right and wrong :

that it is begotten of intolerance and persecution; that it is senseless, besotted, inveterate, and unmerciful; all History teaches us. But perhaps we do not know it in our hearts too well to profit by even so humble an example as the 'No-Popery' riots of seventeen hundred and eighty.

"However imperfectly these disturbances are set forth in the following pages, they are impartially painted by one who has no sympathy with the Romish Church, though he acknowledges, as most men do, some esteemed friends among the followers of its creed."

I have spoke of difficulties which I early foresaw springing up in the course of my task. Such a view now presents itself. Like he to whose memory this tribute is raised, the writer has some esteemed friends among the followers of the Roman Catholic creed, and, moreover, some esteemed, and highly esteemed, friends amongst its clergymen. Doubtless they will appreciate my desire to avoid giving any offence, and will acquit me of the exhibition of any bias partiality in my work of faithfully transcribing what Charles Dickens has to say of Romanism, without gloss or comment of my own.

We naturally, by force of association, turn to the *Pictures from Italy*, and we are not disappointed by lack of material, at all events. With the same unequivocal, and always good-humoured, honesty with which he recorded the plain truth and his deliberate impressions of the Americans, which are often far from flattering, but which the Americans readily forgave for their straightforwardness, and in their admiration of his as bold and fearless denunciation of what he thought was wrong, so, in the *Pictures from Italy*, he as deliberately records the unvarnished truth concerning what he saw and what impression it produced on him. But we will hear his own plea for a fair judgment, made in the first chapter of the book from which I am going to quote:—

"I hope I am not likely to be misunderstood by professors of the Roman Catholic faith, on account of anything contained in these pages. I have done my best, in one of my former productions,* to do justice to them; and I trust, in this, they will do justice to me. When I mention any exhibition that impressed me as absurd or disagreeable, I do not seek to connect it, or recognise it as necessarily connected, with any essentials of their creed. When I treat of the ceremonies of the Holy Week, I merely treat of their effect; and do not challenge the good and learned Dr. Wiseman's interpretation of their

---

* Presumably *Barnaby Rudge*, the whole of which book breathes the spirit of toleration towards the Catholics. More than that, he puts into the mouth of Haredale a plea for justice, and a protest against the unfairness of the movement against them, in the following words:—

"Some of you Protestants of promise are at this moment leagued in yonder building to prevent our having the surpassing and unheard-of privilege of teaching our children to read and write—here—in this land, where thousands of us enter your service every year, and to preserve the freedom of which we die in bloody battles abroad, in heaps: and that others of you, to the number of some thousands, as I learn, are led to look on all men of my creed as wolves and beasts of prey." (Chapter xliii.)

Again, at the commencement of chapter li., we read:—

"The Catholic gentry and tradesmen had no fears for their lives and property, and but little indignation for the wrong they had already sustained in the plunder and destruction of their temples of worship. An honest confidence in the Government under whose protection they had lived for many years, and a well-founded reliance on the good feeling and right thinking of the great mass of the community, with whom, notwithstanding their religious differences, they were every day in the habit of confidential, affectionate, and friendly intercourse, reassured them, even under the excesses that had been committed; and convinced them that they who were Protestants in anything but the name, were no more to be considered as abettors of these disgraceful occurrences, than they themselves were chargeable with the uses of the block, the rack, the gibbet, and the stake in cruel Mary's reign."

In the *American Notes*, too, he makes frequent allusion to the Catholic institutions existing in the States, and, in every instance, commendably and without the slightest trace of bias.

meaning. When I hint a dislike of nunneries for young girls who abjure the world before they have ever proved or known it ; or doubt the *ex officio* sanctity of all Priests and Friars ; I do no more than many conscientious Catholics both abroad and at home."

Accordingly, much of this book, which necessarily has a close association with the religion of the Romish Church, is merely descriptive ; and, being described just as he saw the facts and was impressed by them, is left to produce its own impression on the reader, where another narrator, less tolerant than himself, would have made it a favourable occasion for vindicating his opinions and condemning the religion with which he had no sympathy, and of which, in his private letters, he wrote in the strongest terms of disapprobation.

He is always careful to distinguish between honest faith and mere outward observance, and ever exhibits tender respect for the former, where he believes it to have existed. The very first remark bearing upon the religion of Italy possesses this forbearing tone. He has been writing in his most humorous style of the ludicrous impressions produced upon him by the character of the votive offerings in the chapels at Avignon and elsewhere. He describes them as roughly and comically got up, in a grotesque squareness of outline, and impossibility of perspective, and representative of some sickness or calamity from which the person placing it there had escaped, through the interposition of his or her patron saint, or of the Madonna—

" In one, a lady was having a toe amputated—an operation which a saintly person had sailed into the room, upon a couch, to superintend. In another, a lady was lying in bed, tucked up very tight and prim, and staring with much composure at a tripod, with a slop-basin on it ; the usual form of washing-stand, and the only piece of furniture, besides the bedstead, in her chamber. One would never have supposed her to be suffering from any complaint, beyond the inconvenience of being miraculously wide awake, if the painter had not hit upon the idea of putting all her family on their knees in one corner, with their legs sticking out behind them on the floor, like boot-trees. Above whom, the Virgin, on a kind of blue divan, promised to restore the patient."

But his sense of the ludicrous does not, in this case, obscure his appreciation of the motives which dictated these offerings, for he proceeds to add his recognition of it in the following words :—

"Though votive offerings were not unknown in Pagan temples, and are evidently among the many compromises made between the false religion and the true, when the true was in its infancy, I could wish that all the other compromises were as harmless. Gratitude and Devotion are Christian qualities; and a grateful, humble, Christian spirit may dictate the observance." (Part iii.)

The first point on which he is at open enmity with Romanism—with Romanism of a past day, which, I believe, every true Catholic of this day will cordially join him in condemning for the enormities of its excess—follows immediately upon this, when, on visiting the ancient palace of the Popes at Avignon, he is brought face to face with the remaining evidences of the Inquisition—"the unholy and infamous Inquisition," as he terms it in another place. (*Child's History of England*, chapter xx.) The Chapel of the Holy Office prompts him to speak of the incongruity of the parable of the good Samaritan having been painted on the wall of the chamber,* traceable yet; and he begs his conductress to let him think in silence for five minutes

* This satirical comment will also be found reflecting on Protestantism as well as Catholicism, in Mr. Bumble's parochial buttons, the die of which was the same as the parochial seal—the good Samaritan healing the sick and wounded man—and which he first wore to attend the inquest on the reduced tradesman, who died in a doorway at midnight. (*Oliver Twist*, chapter iv.)

in the chamber of torture, the roof of which is made of such a shape as to stifle the victim's cries!—

"Minutes! seconds are not marked upon the palace clock, when, with her eyes flashing fire, Goblin (*i.e.*, the conductress) is up in the middle of the chamber, describing with her sunburnt arms a wheel of heavy blows. Thus it ran round! cries Goblin. Mash, mash, mash! An endless routine of heavy hammers. Mash, mash, mash! upon the sufferer's limbs. See the stone trough! says Goblin. For the water torture! Gurgle, swill, bloat, burst, for the Redeemer's honour! Suck the bloody rag deep down into your unbelieving body, heretic, at every breath you draw! And when the executioner plucks it out, reeking with the smaller mysteries of God's own image, know us for His chosen servants, true believers in the Sermon on the Mount, elect disciples of Him who never did a miracle but to heal; who never struck a man with palsy, blindness, deafness, dumbness, madness, any one affliction of mankind; and never stretched His blessed hand out but to give relief and ease!"

. . . .

"In October 1791, when the revolution was at its height here, sixty persons, men and women ('and priests,' says Goblin, 'priests'), were murdered, and hurled, the dying and the dead, into the dreadful pit (where the executioner of the Inquisition flung those who were past all further torturing). . . . Was it a portion of the great scheme of retribution that the cruel deed should be committed in this place! . . . They used the Tower of the Forgotten in the name of liberty—their liberty, an earth-born creature in the black mud of the Bastile moats and dungeons, and necessarily betraying many evidences of its unwholesome bringing-up—but the Inquisition used it in the name of heaven."

Finally, gazing into the black, deadly, terrible vaults, in which the prisoners of the Inquisition were immured, and seeing the sun shining in through the decayed and broken wall, he—

"Felt exalted with the proud delight of living in these

degenerate times to see it. The light in the doleful vaults was typical of the light that has streamed in on all persecution, in God's name, but which is not yet at its noon."

Turn we now to section xi., "Rome," and we find a vigorous repetition of his protest against the persecutions which are associated with mediæval Catholicism, suggested by his visit to the Catacombs, the hiding-places of the early Christians, and full of martyrs' graves :—

"When I thought how Christian men have dealt with one another; how, perverting our most merciful religion, they have hunted down and tortured, burnt and beheaded, strangled, slaughtered, and oppressed each other, I pictured to myself an agony surpassing any that this dust had suffered with the breath of life yet lingering in it, and how these great and constant hearts would have been shaken—how they would have quailed and drooped—if a fore-knowledge of the deeds that professing Christians would commit in the Great Name for which they died, could have rent them with its own unutterable anguish on the cruel wheel, and bitter cross, and in the fearful fire."

To these reminiscences of the Romanism of the past may be here added his sentiments on some other accompaniments of its reign. Of excommunication he says :—

"It consisted in declaring the person who was excommunicated an outcast from the Church and from all religious offices; and in cursing him all over, from the top of his head to the sole of his foot, whether he was standing up, lying down, sitting, kneeling, walking, running, hopping, jumping, gaping, coughing, sneezing, or whatever else he was doing. This unchristian nonsense would, of course, have made no sort of difference to the person cursed—who could say his prayers at home if he were shut out of church, and whom none but God could judge." (*Child's History of England*, chapter xii.)

He has no more reverence for the Pope's bull excommunicating Queen Elizabeth, which he terms "a mere dirty piece of paper, not half so powerful as a street ballad" (chapter xxxi.); and, in the same chapter, he cannot reverence a Pope who went in public procession, and had a medal struck to commemorate the "diabolical" massacre of St. Bartholomew, and he declares that "if all the Popes who had ever lived had been rolled into one, they would not have afforded his guilty majesty (Charles the Ninth) the slightest consolation on his deathbed."

Writing of the suppression of the monasteries and abbeys in England, he says :—

"There is no doubt that many of these religious establishments were religious in nothing but name, and were crammed with lazy, indolent, and sensual monks. There is no doubt that they imposed upon the people in every possible way; that they had images moved by wires, which they pretended were miraculously moved by heaven ; that they had among them a whole tun measure full of teeth, all purporting to have come out of the head of one saint, who must indeed have been a very extraordinary person with that enormous allowance of grinders ; that they had bits of coal which they said had fried St. Lawrence, and bits of toe-nails which they said belonged to other famous saints ; penknives, and boots, and girdles, which they said belonged to others ; and that all these bits of rubbish were called relics, and adored by the ignorant people. But, on the other hand, there is no doubt either, that the king's officers and men punished the good monks with the bad ; did great injustice ; demolished many beautiful things and many valuable libraries ; destroyed numbers of fine paintings, stained glass windows, and carvings, and that the whole court were ravenously greedy and rapacious for the division of this great spoil among them. The king seems to have grown almost mad in the ardour of this pursuit ; for he declared Thomas à Becket a traitor, though he had been dead so many years, and had his body dug up out of his grave. He must have been almost as miraculous as the monks pretended, if they had told the truth, for he was found with one head on his shoulders, and they had shown another as his undoubted and genuine head ever since his death ; it had brought them vast sums of money too."
(*Child's History of England*, chapter xxviii.)

He has very little love for monks, at any rate, either ancient or modern. When he describes Leonardo da Vinci's wonderful picture of "The Last Supper" at Milan, he speaks of "a door cut through it by the *intelligent* Dominican friars, to facilitate their operations at dinner time." (*Pictures from Italy*, section x.) Speaking of religious pictures, he makes the following observations:—

"When I observe heads inferior to the subject, in pictures of merit, in Italian galleries, I do not attach that reproach to the painter, for I have a suspicion that these great men, who were of necessity very much in the hands of monks and priests, painted monks and priests a great deal too often. I frequently see, in pictures of real power, heads quite below the story and the painter, *and I invariably observe that these heads are of the convent stamp, and have their counterparts among the convent inmates of this hour;* so, I have settled with myself that, in such cases, the blame was not with the painter, but with the vanity and ignorance of certain of his employers, who would be apostles—on canvas, at all events." (*Pictures from Italy*, section xi.)

The sentiment in italics—a passing and covert reference to modern monks and friars—is deliberately emphasised and enlarged upon in his recollections of Genoa:—

" The streets of Genoa would be all the better for the importation of a few priests of prepossessing appearance. Every fourth or fifth man in the streets is a priest or a monk, and there is pretty sure to be at least one itinerant ecclesiastic inside or outside every hackney coach on the neighbouring roads. I have no knowledge, elsewhere, of more repulsive countenances than are to be found amongst this gentry. If nature's handwriting be at all legible, greater varieties of sloth, deceit, and intellectual torpor could hardly be observed among any class of men in the world.

" Mr. Pepys once heard a clergyman assert in his sermon, in illustration of his respect for the priestly office, that if he could meet a priest and angel together, he would salute the priest first. I am rather of the opinion of Petrarch, who, when his pupil Bocaccio wrote to him, in great tribulation, that he had been visited and admonished for his writings by a Carthusian friar who claimed to be a messenger immediately commissioned by heaven for that purpose, replied, that for his own part he would take the liberty of testing the reality of the commission by personal observation of the messenger's face, eyes, forehead, behaviour, and discourse. I cannot but believe myself, from similar observation, that many unaccredited celestial messengers may be seen skulking through the streets of Genoa, or droning away their lives in other Italian towns.

"Perhaps the Cappucini, though not a learned body, are, as an order, the best friends of the people. They seem to mingle with them more immediately, as their counsellors and comforters; and to go among them more when they are sick; and to pry less than some other orders into the secrets of families, for the purpose of establishing a baleful ascendency over their weaker members; and to be influenced by a less fierce desire to make converts, and, once made, to let them go to ruin, soul and body. They may be seen, in their coarse dress, in all parts of the town at all times, and begging in the markets early in the morning. The Jesuits, too, muster strong in the streets, and go slinking noiselessly about, in pairs, like black cats." (*Pictures from Italy*, section v.)

Of one early example of the genus Monk—St. Dunstan —he writes in uncompromising terms, as a liar, a worker of false miracles, and a villain generally. Of him he says that—

"When he died, the monks settled that he was a saint, and called him Saint Dunstan ever afterwards. They might just as well have settled that he was a coach-horse, and could just as easily have called him one." (*Child's History of England*, chapter iv.)

That it is not the principle of canonisation he condemns, but the principles of the unworthy saints amongst those in the calendar, is evinced by the following commendation :—

"*There are many good and true saints in the calendar*, but San Carlo Borromeo has my warm heart. A charitable doctor to the sick, a munificent friend to the poor, and for this, not in any spirit of blind bigotry, but as the bold opponent of enormous abuses in the Romish Church, I honour his memory. I honour it none the less, because he was nearly slain by a priest, suborned by priests to murder him at the altar, in acknowledgment of his endeavours to reform a false and hypocritical brotherhood of monks." (*Pictures from Italy*, page 340.)

This impartiality is very strongly marked throughout the *Child's History of England*, the most enchantingly written little manual of English history in circulation, and particularly recommendable because of its remarkable freedom from the bias of party-feeling. With him a bad man is a bad man, and his association with reform or commendable policy does not palliate his vices.

"Henry the Eighth," he says, "has been favoured by some Protestant writers, because the Reformation was achieved in his time. But the mighty merit of it lies with other men and not with him; and it can be rendered none the worse by this monster's crimes, and none the better by any defence of them. The plain truth is, that he was a most intolerable ruffian, a disgrace to human nature, and a blot of blood and grease upon the history of England." (*Child's History of England*, chapter xxviii.)

Of Henry the First he writes —

"You may perhaps hear his cunning and promise-breaking called 'policy' by some people, and 'diplomacy' by others. Neither of these fine words will in the least mean that it is true; and nothing that is not true can possibly be good." (*Child's History of England*, chapter x.)

The romance surrounding Richard the First does not dazzle him in pourtraying his character. He sees in him a despicable rebel against his father, a promise-breaker, and a perjurer.

"Richard was said in after years, by way of flattery, to have the heart of a lion. It would have been far better to have had the heart of a man. His heart, whatever it was, had cause to beat remorsefully within his breast, when he came—as he did—into the solemn abbey, and looked on his dead father's uncovered face. His heart, whatever it was, had been a black and perjured heart in all its dealings with the deceased king, and more deficient in a single touch of tenderness than any wild beast's in the forest." (*Child's History of England*, chapter xii., part ii.)

The history of Queen Mary's reign he concludes with these words:—

"As bloody Queen Mary this woman has become famous, and as bloody Queen Mary she will ever be justly remembered with horror and detestation in Great Britain. Her memory has been held in such abhorrence that some writers have arisen in later years to take her part, and to show that she was, upon the whole, quite an amiable and cheerful sovereign! 'By their fruits ye shall know them,' said Our Saviour. The stake and the fire were the fruits of this reign, and you will judge this Queen by nothing else." (*Child's History of England*, chapter xxx.)

Of Charles the First he says:—

"With all my sorrow for him, I cannot agree with him that he died 'the martyr of the people;' for the people had been martyrs to him, and to his ideas of a king's rights, long before." (*Child's History of England*, conclusion of chapter xxxiii.)

Returning for a moment to Catholic saints, we find that he has little sympathy with the adulation paid to them by the faithful, or the mediatory power assigned to them or to their remains by the Church. He tells us the story of Harold being sworn on the missal, which was placed on a tub, which tub was shown him to be full of dead saints' bones, which it was supposed made his oath a great deal more impressive and binding. "As if," he adds, significantly, "the great name of the Creator of Heaven and earth could be made more solemn by a knuckle-bone, or a double-tooth, or a finger-nail of Dunstan." (*Child's History of England*, chapter vi.)

In *Pictures from Italy* he alludes to the well-known sacred blood of San Gennaro or Januarius, a modern relic which excites somewhat the same reverence in Naples now as St. Dunstan's bones did in the time of Harold. He says:—

"It is preserved in two phials in a silver tabernacle, and miraculously liquefies three times a-year, to the great admiration of the people. At the same moment, the stone (distant some miles) where the saint suffered martyrdom becomes faintly red. It is said that the officiating priest turns faintly red also, sometimes, when these miracles occur." (Section xii.— A Rapid Diorama.)

His reverence is not excited by the "externals" which are designed by the church to excite the devotion of Christians. He speaks of his "postillion, concentrated essence of all the shabbiness in Italy," touching his hat to "a blunt-nosed little virgin, hardly less shabby than himself, enshrined in a plaster Punch's show." (*Pictures from Italy*, section vi.—Parma, Modena, and Bologna.) Speaking of the Genoese churches, while he expresses a keen appreciation of that which is really splendid and artistic, he says that they are "set, side by side, with sprawling effigies of maudlin monks, and the veriest trash and tinsel ever seen." (Section v.—Genoa.)

One of the raciest bits in this book, and which I think my Catholic friends will forgive me for quoting, if only for its keen sense of humour, is that of a congregation at mass being disturbed by a gorgeous circus procession:—

"When the procession had so entirely passed away, that the shrill trumpet was mild in the distance, and the tail of the last horse was hopelessly round the corner, the people who had come out of the church to stare at it went back again. But one old lady, kneeling on the pavement within, near the door, had seen it all, and had been immensely interested, without getting up; and this old lady's eye, at that juncture, I happened to catch : to our mutual confusion. She cut our embarrassment very short, however, by crossing herself devoutly, and going down, at full length, on her face, before a figure in a fancy petticoat and a gilt crown; which was so like one of the procession figures, that perhaps at this hour she may think the whole appearance a celestial vision. Anyhow, I must certainly have forgiven her her interest in the circus, though I had been her father confessor." (*Pictures from Italy*, section vi.—Parma, Modena, and Bologna.)

"But of all the dangerous reliance on outward observances," he writes, in the same volume, " in themselves mere empty forms, none struck me half so much as the Scala Sancta, or Holy Staircase."

" This holy staircase is composed of eight and twenty steps, said to have belonged to Pontius Pilate's house, and to be the identical stairs on which our Saviour trod, in coming down from the judgment-seat. Pilgrims ascend it only on their knees. It is steep ; and at the summit is a chapel, reported to be full of relics, into which they peep through some iron bars, and then come down again by one of two side staircases, which are not sacred, and may be walked on. On Good Friday there were, on a moderate computation, a hundred people slowly shuffling up these stairs on their knees at one time ; while others who were going up, or had come down—and a few who had done both, and were going up again for the second time—stood loitering in the porch below, where an old gentleman in a sort of watch-box rattled a tin canister, with a slit in the top, incessantly, to remind them that he took the money. The majority were country people, male and female. There were four or five Jesuit priests, however, and some half-dozen well-dressed women. A whole school of boys, twenty at least, were about half-way up—evidently enjoying it very much. They

CHAPTER V.

What he objects to in Religious practice—(continued).

HOUGH he had "no sympathy with the Romish Church," he does not play Protestantism off against it, but as we have already seen, in our review of the No-Popery Riots, has as little sympathy with the latter when it falls into error. His strong leanings to the Church of England has been noted, but they were not so strong as to obscure his view of abuses therein.

When Squeers examines the papers stolen from Arthur Gride, he comes across a deed of sale of the right of presentation to the rectory of Purechurch, in the valley of Cashup, and he cautions his accomplice to take care of that, literally for God's sake, as it'll fetch its price at the Auction Mart. (*Nicholas Nickleby*, chapter lvii.)

The brutal and drunken country justice in *Barnaby Rudge* is described as warmly attached to church and state, and as never appointing to the living in his gift any but a three-bottle man and a first rate fox-hunter. (Chapter xlvii.)

Speaking of King John unwillingly recompensing the clergy, after his reconciliation with the Pope, for the losses he had caused them, he says :—

"The end of it was, that the superior clergy got a good deal, and the inferior clergy got little or nothing—which has also happened since King John's time, I believe." (*Child's History of England*, chapter xlv.)

That is a most delicately skilful picture which is drawn of a Protestant dignitary in *Little Dorrit*—the pliant and adaptable Bishop magnate, the ecclesiastical lion of Mr. Merdle's dinners. His maintenance of his ecclesiastical propriety in the trying atmosphere of society, and his reconcilement of Mr. Merdle's wealth (with the worship it begot) with what the religion of which he is the high-priest has to say about that subject, is the finest of satires. Chapter xxi. of book i., and chapter xii. of book ii. require to be read through to fully appreciate it, but a few extracts may advantageously come in this place:—

"Bishop said he was glad to think this wealth flowed into the coffers of a gentleman who was always disposed to maintain the best interests of society." (That is, the lavish dinners, the worldliness, and the jewels on Mrs. Merdle's bosom.)

"Bishop said he was glad to think that this wealth flowed into the coffers of a gentleman who accepted it with meekness." (The meekness of a rogue's conscience, as the sequel proved.)

"Bishop then came undesignedly sliding in the direction of the sideboard.

"'Surely the goods of this world,' it occurred in an accidental way to Bishop to remark, 'could scarcely be directed into happier channels than when they accumulated under the magic touch of the wise and sagacious, who, while they knew the just value of riches (Bishop tried here to look as if he were rather poor himself), were aware of their importance, judiciously governed and rightly distributed, to the welfare of our brethren at large.'

"Mr. Merdle with humility expressed his conviction that Bishop couldn't mean him, and with inconsistency expressed his high gratification in Bishop's good opinion.

"Bishop then—jauntily stepping out a little with his well-shaped right leg, as though he said to Mr. Merdle, 'Don't mind the apron; a mere form!'*—put this case to his good friend:

"Whether it had occurred to his good friend that society might not unreasonably hope that one so blest in his undertakings, and whose example on his pedestal was so influential with it, would shed a little money in the direction of a mission or so to Africa?

"Mr. Merdle signifying that the idea should have his best attention, Bishop put another case:

"Whether his good friend had at all interested himself in the proceedings of our Combined Additional Endowed Dignitaries Committee, and whether it had occurred to him that to shed a little money in *that* direction might be a great conception finely executed?

"Mr. Merdle made a similar reply, and Bishop explained reason for inquiring.

"Society looked to such men as his good friend to do such things. It was not that *he* looked to them, but that society looked to them. Just as it was not Our Committee who wanted the Additional Endowed Dignitaries, but it was society that was in a state of the most agonising uneasiness of mind until it got them. He begged to assure his good friend that he was extremely sensible of his good friend's regard on all occasions for the best interests of society; and he considered that he was at once consulting those interests, and expressing the feeling of society, when he wished him continued prosperity, continued increase of riches, and continued things in general."

"Bishop had no idea that there was anything significant in the occasion. That was the most remarkable trait in his character. He was crisp, fresh, cheerful, affable, bland; but so surprisingly innocent."

"The agreeable young Barnacle, and Bar, were the talkers of the party. Bishop would have been exceedingly agreeable also,

* "Dignity, and even holiness, too, sometimes, are more questions of coat and waistcoat than some people imagine." (*Oliver Twist*, chapter xxxvii.)

but that his innocence stood in his way. He was so soon left behind. When there was any little hint of anything being in the wind, he got lost directly. Worldly affairs were too much for him; he couldn't make them out at all."

But while Bishop is thus twitted for his trimming, in his attempts to reconcile society's shortcomings and religion's duty to society, Dickens was an inveterate foe to that perversion of religion which seeks to repress all that is happy and pleasant in life, to frown down all innocent mirth and recreation, and to make the service of God an austere and irksome thing.

In speaking of the Puritans in the *Child's History of England*, he characterises them as " for the most part an uncomfortable people, who thought it highly meritorious to dress in a hideous manner, talk through their noses, and oppose all harmless enjoyments " (chapter xxxi.); and in the account of the sermon in the London theatre, he advises those who preside over such assemblies, not to disparage the places in which they speak, nor to set themselves in antagonism to the natural desire of the mass of mankind to recreate themselves and to be amused. He gives fuller expression to these sentiments in *Barnaby Rudge*, where the gleeful idiot yields to the impulses of his wayward nature, and runs, and climbs, and hides, that he may leap out and startle his mother, or whatever else it prompted him.

"It is something to look upon enjoyment, so that it be free and wild and in the face of nature, though it is but the enjoyment of an idiot. It is something to know that heaven has left the capacity of gladness in such a creature's breast; it is something to be assured that, however lightly men may crush that faculty in their fellows, the Great Creator of mankind imparts it even to his despised and slighted work. Who would not rather see a poor idiot happy in the sunlight, than a wise man pining in a darkened jail?

"Ye men of gloom and austerity, who paint the face of Infinite Benevolence with an eternal frown; read in the Everlasting Book, wide open to your view, the lesson it would teach. Its pictures are not in black and sombre hues, but bright and glowing tints; its music—save when ye drown it—is not in sighs and groans, but songs and cheerful sounds. Listen to the million voices in the summer air, and find one as dismal as your own. Remember, if ye can, the sense of hope and pleasure which every glad return of day awakens in the breast of all your kind who have not changed their nature; and learn some wisdom even from the witless, when their hearts are lifted up, they know not why, by all the mirth and happiness it brings." (Chapter xxv.)

Mr. and Miss Murdstone and Mrs. Clennam are the most striking personifications of this austere creed. In an early chapter of *David Copperfield* we have the description of the severe way in which the Murdstones used to go to church, and the cruel relish with which the sister emphasised the dread words in the responses. Little Dr. Chillip is reintroduced in chapter lix., to further define their religion, and to mark the author's disapprobation of the principles of those of whom they are the portraiture—

"'Does he gloomily profess to be (I am ashamed to use the word in such association) religious still?' I inquired.

"'You anticipate, sir,' said Mr. Chillip . . . 'one of Mrs. Chillip's most impressive remarks. Mrs. Chillip . . . quite electrified me by pointing out that Mr. Murdstone sets up an image of himself, and calls it the Divine Nature. . . . Mr. Murdstone delivers public addresses sometimes, and it is said—in short, sir, it is said by Mrs. Chillip—that the darker tyrant he has lately been, the more ferocious is his doctrine. . . . Mrs. Chillip goes so far as to say, that what people miscall their religion is a vent for their bad humours and arrogance. And do you know I must say, sir, that I *don't* find authority for Mr. and Miss Murdstone in the New Testament? . . . In the meantime they are much disliked; and as they are very free in consigning everybody who dislikes them to perdition, we really have a good deal of perdition going on in our neighbourhood.'"

In a much earlier volume, one of the series presumed to belong to the time of his undefined religious views, he marks his disapprobation of the stern gospel whose mainstay is vengeance, and, by contrast, his interpretation of the true gospel as one of mercy and forgiveness :—

"'Your haughty religious people would have held their heads up to see me as I am to-night, and preached of flames and vengeance,' cried Nancy. 'Oh, dear lady, why arn't those who claim to be God's own folks as gentle and kind to us poor wretches as you, who, having youth, and beauty, and all that they have lost, might be a little proud instead of so much humbler?'

"'Ah,' said the gentleman, 'a Turk turns his face, after washing it well, to the East, when he says his prayers; these good people, after giving their faces such a rub against the world as to take the smiles off, turn with no less regularity to the darkest side of heaven. Between the Mussulman and the Pharisee, commend me to the first!'" (*Oliver Twist*, chapter xlvi.)

But it is the remarkable conception of Mrs. Clennam which most fully and minutely developes his sentiments on, and most earnestly and pointedly repudiates this, to him, obnoxious creed. I have always thought Mrs. Clennam to be one of the most carefully wrought-up characters in his books, the result of close observation of the class of whom she is a representative, and of deliberate and skilful analysis of their doctrine, and, it may be added, of studious comparison with the religion of the Bible, where, as in the case of the Murdstones, he finds no warrant for them. Arthur Clennam, reviewing the miserable Sundays of his early days, thinks of the time when—

"His mother, stern of face and unrelenting of heart, would sit all day behind a Bible—bound, like her own construction of it, in the hardest, barest, and straightest boards, with one dinted ornament on the cover like the drag of a chain, and a wrathful sprinkling of red upon the edges of the leaves—as if it, of all books! were a fortification against sweetness of temper, natural affection, and gentle intercourse." (*Little Dorrit*, book i., chapter iii.)

That she makes it so, though, is obvious when—

"She put on the spectacles and reads certain passages—sternly, fiercely, wrathfully—praying that her enemies (she made them by her tone and manner expressly hers) might be put to the edge of the sword, consumed by fire, smitten by plagues and leprosy, that their bones might be ground to dust, and that they might be utterly exterminated." (*Ibid.*)

So again, when offended by her son's hinted suspicions, she puts two fingers between its leaves, and closing the book upon them, holds it up to him in a threatening way, and says:—

"'In the days of old, Arthur, treated of in this commentary, there were pious men, beloved of the Lord, who would have cursed their sons for less than this: who would have sent them forth, and sent whole nations forth, if such had supported them, to be avoided of God and man, and perish, down to the baby at the breast. But I only tell you that if you ever renew that theme with me I will renounce you; I will so dismiss you through that doorway, that you had better have been motherless from your cradle. I will never see or know you more. And if, after all, you were to come into this darkened room to look upon me lying dead, my body should bleed, if I could make it, when you came near me.'

"In part relieved by the intensity of this threat, and in part (monstrous as the fact is) by a general impression that it was in some sort a religious proceeding . . . " (Book i., chapter v.)

Such is the unsympathetic and unchristian professor of religion, as painted in her own words. In an earlier part of the book her religious character is defined and stamped with reprehension by her son, who says to Mr. Meagles—

"I am the only child of parents who weighed, measured, and priced everything; for whom what could not be weighed, measured, and priced, had no existence. Strict people, as the phrase is, professors of a stern religion, their very religion was a gloomy sacrifice of tastes and sympathies that were never their own, offered up as a part of a bargain for the security of their possessions. Austere faces, inexorable discipline, penance in this world and terror in the next—nothing graceful or gentle anywhere, and the void in my cowed heart everywhere—this was my childhood, if I may so misuse the word as to apply it to such a beginning of life." (Book i., chapter ii.)

Further, that there may be no misapprehension of the moral to be enforced, we have the following diatribe:—

"Woe to the supplicant, if such a one were or ever had been, who had any concession to look for in the inexorable face at the cabinet. Woe to the defaulter whose appeal lay to the tribunal where those severe eyes presided. Great need had the rigid woman of her mystical religion, veiled in gloom and darkness, with lightnings of cursing, vengeance, and destruction, flashing through the sable clouds. Forgive us our debts as we forgive our debtors was a prayer too poor in spirit for her. Smite Thou my debtors, Lord, wither them, crush them; do Thou as I would do, and Thou shalt have my worship. This was the impious tower of stone she built up to scale heaven." (Book i., chapter v.)

One noticeable feature in her religious composition is that which has been already alluded to, and which is characteristic of Chadband, Pecksniff, and Hawkyard, immortal triad of hypocrites. Truly, Mrs. Clennam is only one remove from a hypocrite herself, and carries with her into the creed which she has imposed upon herself as righteousness the same distinguishing mark so strongly developed in them. It is that of keeping a debtor and creditor account with the Majesty of Heaven, posting up the entries to her credit, strictly keeping her set-off, and claiming her due. Thus, she speaks of her reparation for fifteen years, in the room in which she has voluntarily immured herself, and which she says she endures without murmuring. (Chapter v.) In another place she speaks of leading a life of self-correction, and of having offences to expiate, and peace to make. (Chapter xxx.) A selection from this chapter is worth making in this place, in which she is made to speak thus:—

"'I shape my course by pilots, strictly by proved and true pilots, under whom I cannot be shipwrecked—cannot be—and that if I were unmindful of the admonition conveyed in these three letters, I should not be half as chastened as I am.'

"It was curious how she seized the occasion to argue with some invisible opponent. Perhaps with her own better sense, always turning upon herself and her own deception.

"'If I forgot my ignorance in my life of health and freedom, I might complain of the life to which I am now condemned. I never do. I never have done. If I forget that this scene, the earth, is expressly meant to be a scene of gloom, and hardship, and dark trial, for the creatures who are made out of its dust, I might have some tenderness for its vanities. But I have no such tenderness. If I did not know that we are, every one, the subject (most justly the subject) of a wrath that must be satisfied, and against whom mere actions are nothing, I might repine at the difference between me, imprisoned here, and the people who pass that gateway yonder. But I take it as a grace and favour to be elected to make the satisfaction I am working here, to know what I know for certain here, and to work out what I have worked out here. My affliction might otherwise have had no meaning for me. Hence I would forget, and I do forget, nothing. Hence I am contented, and say it is better with me than with millions.'"

Still more deeply is this character analysed, its formation and growth marked, its impious possibilities exhibited, and its monstrousness unmistakably branded, in the account of her last interview with Rigaud, when she is finally brought to bay.

"'You do not know what it is,' she went on, 'to be brought up strictly and straitly. I was so brought up. Mine was no light youth of sinful gaiety and pleasure. Mine were days of wholesome repression, punishment, and fear. The corruption of our hearts, the evil of our ways, the curse that is upon us, the terrors that surround us—these were the themes of my childhood. They formed my character, and filled me with an abhorrence of evil-doers. When old Mr. Gilbert Clennam proposed his orphan nephew to my father for my husband, my father impressed upon me that his bringing-up had been, like mine, one of severe restraint. He told me that besides the discipline his spirit had undergone, he lived in a starved house, where rioting and gaiety were unknown, and where every day was a day of toil and trial like the last. He told me that he had been a man in years long before his uncle had acknowledged him as one; and that, from his school-days to that hour, his uncle's roof had been a sanctuary to him from the contagion of the irreligious and dissolute. When, within a twelvemonth of our marriage, I found my husband, at that time when my father spoke of him, to have sinned against the Lord, and outraged me by holding a guilty creature in my place, was I to doubt that it had been appointed to me to make the discovery, and that it was appointed to me to lay the hand of punishment upon that creature of perdition? Was I to dismiss in a moment—not my own wrongs—what was I? but all the rejection of sin, and all the war against it, in which I had been bred? . . . Was it my own wrong I remembered? Mine! I was but a servant and a minister. What power could I have had over them, but that they were bound in the bonds of their sin, and delivered over to me!'

"More than forty years had passed over the grey head of this determined woman since the time she recalled. More than forty years of strife and struggle with the whisper that, by whatever name she called her vindictive pride and rage, nothing through all eternity could change their nature. Yet, gone those more than forty years, and come this Nemesis now looking her in the face, she still abided by her old impiety—still reversed the order of Creation, and breathed her own breath into a clay image of her Creator. Verily, verily, travellers have seen many monstrous idols in many countries; but no human eyes have ever seen more daring, gross, and shocking images of the divine nature, than we creatures of the dust make in our own likenesses of our own bad passions.

"'When I forced him to give her up to me, by her name and place of abode,' she went on; 'when I accused her, and she fell hiding her face at my feet, was it my injury that I asserted, were they my reproaches that I poured upon her? Those who were appointed of old to go to wicked kings and accuse them— were they not ministers and servants? And had not I, unworthy and far removed from them, sin to denounce? When she pleaded to me her youth, and his wretched and hard life (that was her phrase for the virtuous training he had belied), and the desecrated ceremony of marriage there had been between them, and the terrors of want and shame that had overwhelmed them both when I was first appointed to be the instrument of their punishment, and the love (for she said the word to me, down at my feet) in which she had abandoned him and left him to me, was it *my* enemy that became my footstool, were they the words of *my* wrath that made her shrink and quiver? Not unto me the strength be ascribed; not unto me the wringing of the expiation! . . . And what was the repentance that was extorted from the hardness of her heart and the blackness of her depravity? . . . She had to sacrifice her sinful and shameful affections; no more. She was then free to bear her load of guilt in secret, and to break her heart in secret; and through such present misery (light enough for her, I think!) to purchase her redemption from endless misery, if she could. If, in this, I punished her here, did I not open to her a way hereafter? If she knew herself to be surrounded by insatiable vengeance and unquenchable fires, were they mine? If I threatened her, then and afterwards, with the terrors that encompassed her, did I hold them in my right hand! . . . It is appointed against such offences that the offenders shall not be able to forget. . . . As well might it be charged upon me, that the stings of an awakened conscience drove her mad, and that it was the will of the Disposer of all things that she should live so, many years. I devoted myself to reclaim the otherwise predestined and lost boy; to give him the reputation of an honest origin; to bring him up in fear and trembling, and in a life of practical contrition for the sins that were heavy on his head before his entrance into this condemned world.'" (Book ii., chapter xxx.)

How pointed a comment on her warped and embittered religion the simple words of Little Dorrit are, in the next chapter. The very innocence and self-sacrificing constancy of the latter, in strong contrast to the self-deception and inflexible hardness of the former, is in itself a rebuke. Those words, and the expressions which call them forth, will fitly point the moral:—

"'I have done,' said Mrs. Clennam, 'what it was given me to do. I have set myself against evil; not against good. I have been an instrument of severity against sin. Have not mere sinners like myself been commissioned to lay it low in all time? ... Even if my own wrong had prevailed with me, and my own vengeance had moved me, could I have found no justification? None in the old days, when the innocent perished with the guilty, a thousand to one? When the wrath of the hater of the unrighteous was not slaked even in blood, and yet found favour?'

"'Oh, Mrs. Clennam, Mrs. Clennam,' said Little Dorrit, 'angry feelings and unforgiving deeds are no comfort and no guide to you and me. My life has been passed in this poor prison, and my teaching has been very defective, but let me implore you to remember later and better days. Be guided only by the Healer of the sick, the Raiser of the dead, the Friend of all who were afflicted and forlorn, the patient Master who shed tears of compassion for our infirmities. We cannot but be right if we put all the rest away, and do everything in remembrance of Him. There is no vengeance and no infliction of suffering in His life, I am sure. There can be no confusion in following Him, and seeking for no other footsteps, I am certain!'

"In the softened light of the window, looking from the scene of her early trials to the shining sky, she was not in stronger opposition to the black figure in the shade, than the life and doctrine on which she rested were to that figure's history." (Book ii., chapter xxxi.)

There is another kind of misdirected zeal upon which Dickens is severely satirical, as set forth in the delineation of the Jellyby family and Mrs. Pardiggle.

We are made to feel, as soon as we set foot in the Jellyby mansion, that there is something radically wrong therein. The tarnished plate-door and neglected and dirty Peepy, with his head imprisoned between the area railings, prepare us for further discomforts within, which comprehend a graphic picture of a most utterly neglected home. Caddy, with not an article of dress upon her, from a pin upwards, that is in its proper condition or its right place; Mr. Jellyby, without a word to say for himself, and without anybody to say a word to him or to trouble themselves about him; the young woman with a swelled face bound up in a flannel bandage, blowing the fire of the drawing-room, and choking dreadfully, and again performing the same duty next morning with a smutty parlour candlestick—throwing in the candle to make it burn better, while everything is as left overnight, and evidently intended to remain so; the dinner an hour late, and almost raw, with the flannel-bandaged young woman dropping everything on the table wherever it happened to go, and never moving it again till she put it on the stairs; no hot water forthcoming for ablutionary purposes because the kettle is mislaid and the boiler out of order; the window-curtain fastened up with a fork; and crumbs, dust, and waste paper all over the house, especially the latter, in the sanctum of Mrs. Jellyby, the abstracted and serene source of all the confusion, the "Borriobhoola-Gha" enthusiast, the woman with a mission, with unkempt hair, and her dress not nearly meeting up the back, and the open space railed across with a lattice-work of stay-lace, like a summer-house. The African project, she says, employs her whole time, to the total exclusion of her home projects, as the above description tells us. It involves her in correspondence with individuals anxious for the welfare of their species, she says, while her own family are ignored. It brings Mr. Quale, with his shining knobs for temples, and his philanthropy and loquacity, to hold discussions on the Brotherhood of Humanity, while the relations of a wife are dead and spurned. The book does not say so in words, but the inference is obvious enough, and the reproof a severe one. (*Bleak House*, chapter iv.)

Mrs. Pardiggle is but another variety of the woman with a mission. She is a school lady; she is a visiting lady; she is a reading lady; she is a distributing lady; she is on the local linen box committee, and many general committees; and her canvassing alone is very extensive—perhaps no one's more so. She is a formidable style of lady, with spectacles, a prominent nose, and a loud voice, who doesn't know what fatigue is. We are not introduced into her home, but we are introduced to her family, and are enabled to note a point of divergence from Mrs. Jellyby's system, insomuch that her young family are not excluded from participation in the objects to which she is devoted, but she takes them everywhere, and makes them participate in all her projects. But it is a matter for nice adjudication whether Mrs. Jellyby's family haven't the best of it, after all, seeing that the young Pardiggles' pocket-money is confiscated for the benefit of the Tockahoopo Indians, the Superannuated Widows, and the Grand National Smithers Testimonial, that they are dragged out at half-past six on winter's mornings to attend matins, and that they are steamed in the breath of sundry "Boanerges Boilers" for two hours together. We are taken upon one of Mrs. Pardiggle's rounds, where she leads the way with a great show of moral determination, and takes the families into religious custody, as if she were an inexorable moral policeman.

"She certainly did make, in this, as in everything else, a

show that was not conciliatory, of doing Charity by wholesale, and of dealing in it to a large extent." (*Bleak House*, chapter vii.)

Here again Dickens characteristically marks his disapprobation of the Pardiggle proceedings by force of contrast. Her ministrations, however well meant, produce more harm than good: they cause the bricklayer whom she exercises them on to be abusive, and his family to take no notice whatever, excepting when the young man made the dog bark (which he usually did when Mrs. Pardiggle was most emphatic). As to the little book which she left for their edification, Mr. Jarndyce said he doubted if Robinson Crusoe could have read it though he had had no other on his desolate island.

But when Mrs. Pardiggle leaves the room, and Ada and Esther are left behind, they approach the woman sitting by the fire, to ask if the baby is ill—

"Ada, whose gentle heart was moved by its appearance, bent down to touch its little face. As she did so, I saw what had happened and drew her back. The child died. . . . Such compassion, such gentleness, as that with which she bent down weeping, and put her hand upon the mother's, might have softened any mother's heart that ever beat. The woman at first gazed at her in astonishment, and then burst into tears.

"Presently I took the light burden from her lap; did what I could to make the baby's rest the prettier and gentler; laid it on a shelf, and covered it with my own handkerchief. We tried to comfort the mother, and we whispered to her what Our Saviour said of childen. She answered nothing, but sat weeping—weeping very much.

"When I turned, I found that the young man had taken out the dog, and was standing at the door looking in upon us; with dry eyes, but quiet. The girl was quiet too, and sat in a corner looking upon the ground. The man had risen. He still smoked his pipe with an air of defiance, but he was silent." (*Ibid.*)

Mrs. Weller's last words, as reported by her bereaved

husband, contain an emphatic comment upon Mrs. Jellyby and Pardiggle and the class they represent :—

"'Veller,' she says, 'I'm afeard I've not done by you quite wot I ought to ha' done; you're a wery kind-hearted man, and I might ha' made your home more comfortabler. I begin to see now,' she says, 'ven its too late, that if a married 'ooman wishes to be religious, she should begin with dischargin' her dooties at home, and makin' them as is about her cheerful and happy, and that vile she goes to church, or chapel, or wot not, at all proper times, she should be wery careful not to con-wert this sort o' thing into a excuse for idleness or self-indulgence.'" (Chapter lii.)

Jo, in *Bleak House*, is made the medium for a skilful diagnosis of Jellyby-Pardiggle missionary enterprise, in which, if the criticism is a little severe, a good deal of truth will be recognised :—

"Jo is brought in. He is not of Mrs. Pardiggle's Tockahoopo Indians; he is not one of Mrs. Jellyby's lambs, being wholly unconnected with Borriobhoola-Gha; he is not softened by distance and unfamiliarity, he is not a genuine foreign-grown savage; he is the ordinary home-made article. Dirty, ugly, disagreeable, to all the senses, in body a common creature of the common streets, only in soul a heathen. Homely filth begrimes him, parasites devour him, homely sores are in him, homely rags are on him; native ignorance, the growth of English soil and climate, sinks his immortal nature lower than the beasts that perish. Stand forth, Jo, in uncompromising colours! From the sole of thy foot to the crown of thy head, there is nothing interesting about thee." (Chapter xlvii.)

There will be some people ready to construe this into a sneer at missionary zeal. That he certainly did not deprecate true sacrifice in that cause is obvious when he speaks of Livingstone, whom he characterises "that model missionary and good brave man." (*Uncommercial Traveller*, chapter xxvi.)

CHAPTER VI.

Charles Dickens on Christian Doctrine.

WE have seen, so far, what Charles Dickens approved of and what he disapproved of in Christian practice, and gained a clue to his own religious character in the inquiry. It will be my province now to endeavour to show that his admiration for the one, and his strictures on the other, were based on no uncertain grounds, but that his views were the emanation of definite convictions, in the certainty of which he spoke with authority. This, the actual fulfilment of the investigation promised by the title, is commended to the fair judgment of my readers, and the highest reward coveted is to add to the already long list of the admirers of Dickens, by showing the claim he has upon the sympathies of those who are anxious to put Christian reading into the hands of their children, pupils, and dependants. For I hope to prove that the soundness of his Christianity, as well as of his morality, commend his writings to rank high in the select department of religious educative literature, while they take the lead amongst works of fiction in commending themselves to the hearty appreciation of the reading public, religious and non-religious, as a happy combination of advantages which all who desire the advancement of true religion must see to promise the happiest results.

His writings yield copious sentiments on all the essential doctrines of Christianity, and it will be the clearest and most convenient way to arrange them under their various headings, and, as far as possible, in the chronological order in which they were written. The most voluminous comes under the heading of that great truth which is at the root of all religion,

IMMORTALITY.

The Old Curiosity Shop yields the following testimonies:—

". . . Said the child, 'I used to read to him by the fireside, and he sat listening, and when I stopped and we began to talk, he told me about my mother, and how she once looked and spoke just like me when she was a little child. Then he used to take me on his knee and try to make me understand that she was not lying in her grave, but had flown to a beautiful country beyond the sky, where nothing died, or ever grew old. . . .'" (Chapter vi.)

" How many of the mounds in that old churchyard where she had lately strayed grew green above the graves of children! And though she thought as a child herself, and did not perhaps sufficiently consider to what a bright and happy existence those who die young are borne. . . . Her dreams were of the little scholar: not coffined and covered up, but mingling with angels, and smiling happily." (Chapter xxvi.)

" He was a very young boy; quite a little child. His hair still hung in curls about his face, and his eyes were very bright; but their light was of heaven, not earth." (Chapter xxv.)

" Oh! the glory of the sudden burst of light; the freshness of the fields and woods, stretching away on every side, and meeting the bright blue sky; the cattle grazing in the pasturage; the smoke, that, coming from among the trees, seemed to rise upward from the green earth; the children yet at their gambols down below—all, everything, so beautiful and happy! It was like passing from death to life; it was drawing nearer heaven." (Chapter liii.)

"'There is nothing,' cried the schoolmaster, 'no, nothing innocent or good, that dies and is forgotten. Let us hold to that faith, or none. An infant, a prattling child, dying in its cradle, will live again in the better thoughts of those who loved it, and will play its part through them, in the redeeming actions of the world, though its body be burnt to ashes or drowned in the deepest sea. There is not an angel added to the host of heaven but does its blessed work on earth in those that loved it here. Forgotten! Oh, if the good deeds of human creatures could be traced to their source, how beautiful would even death appear; for how much charity, mercy, and purified affliction would be seen to have their growth in dusty graves.'" (Chapter liv.)

"'Why, they say,' replied the boy, looking up into her face, 'that you will be an angel before the birds sing again. But you won't be, will you? Don't leave us, Nell, though the sky *is* bright. Do not leave us!... After a time, the kind angels will be glad to think that you are not among them, and that you stayed here to be with us. Willie went away to join them. ... They say that Willie is in heaven now, and that it's always summer there. ... But if you do go, Nell, be fond of him for my sake. Tell him how I love him still, and how much I loved you; and when I think that you two are together, and are happy, I'll try to bear it, and never give you pain by doing wrong—indeed, I never will!'. . .

"——There was a tearful silence, but it was not long before she looked upon him with a smile, and promised him, in a gentle, quiet voice, that she would stay and be his friend as long as heaven would let her." (Chapter lv.)

"For she was dead. . . . Where were the traces of her early cares, her sufferings, and fatigues? All gone. Sorrow was dead indeed in her, but peace and perfect happiness were born: imaged in her tranquil beauty and profound repose.

"And still her former self lay there, unaltered in this change.

"Yes. The old fireside had smiled upon that same sweet face; it had passed, like a dream, through haunts of misery and care; at the door of the poor schoolmaster on the summer evening, before the furnace fire upon the cold wet night, at the still bedside of the dying boy, there had been the same mild lovely look. So shall we know the angels in their majesty, after death. . . .

"'It is not,' said the schoolmaster, as he bent down to kiss her on the cheek, and gave his tears free vent, 'it is not on earth that heaven's justice ends. Think what earth is, compared to the world to which her young spirit has winged its flight; and say, if one deliberate wish expressed in solemn terms above this bed could call her back to life, which of us would utter it.'" (Chapter lxxi.)

"'It is a good and happy sleep, eh?'
"'Indeed it is,' returned the bachelor. 'Indeed, indeed it is.'
"'That's well!—and the waking——' faltered the old man.
"'Happy too. Happier than tongue can tell, or heart of man conceive.'" (Chapter lxxi.)

"Waking, she never wandered in her mind but once, and that was of beautiful music which she said was in the air. God knows. It may have been." (Chapter lxxii.)

"They saw the vault covered, and the stone fixed down. Then, when the dusk of evening had come on, and not a sound disturbed the sacred stillness of the place—when the bright moon poured in her light on tomb and monument, on pillar, wall, and arch, and most of all (it seemed to them) upon her quiet grave—in that calm time, *when outward things teem with evidences of immortality*, and worldly hopes and fears are humbled in the dust before them—then, with tranquil and submissive hearts, they turned away, and left the child with God." (Chapter lxxii.)

From *American Notes*:—

" . . . I sat down in another room, before a girl, blind, deaf, and dumb. . . . There she was, before me; built up, as it were, in a marble cell, impervious to any ray of light or particle of sound ; with her poor white hand peeping through a chink in the wall, beckoning to some good man for help, that an immortal soul might be awakened." (Chapter iii.)

"I recollect when I was a very young child having a fancy that the reflection of the moon in water was a path to heaven ; and this old feeling came over me again, when I watched it on a tranquil night at sea." (Chapter xvi.)

From *Dombey and Son:*—

"'Once upon a time,' said Richards, 'there was a lady—a very good lady—and her little daughter dearly loved her. . . . Who, when God thought it right that it should be so, was taken ill and died. . . . Died, never to be seen again by anyone on earth, and was buried in the ground where the trees grow . . . where the ugly little seeds turn into beautiful flowers, and into grass, and corn, and I don't know what all besides. Where good people turn into bright angels, and fly away to heaven. . . . So, when this lady died, wherever they took her, or wherever they put her, she went to God! and she prayed to Him, this lady did, to teach her little daughter to be sure of that in her heart ; and to know that she was happy there and loved her still ; and to hope and try—oh, all her life—to meet her there one day, never, never, never to part any more.'" (Chapter ii.)

From *Bleak House:*—

"He slowly laid his face down upon her bosom, drew his arms closer round her neck, and with one parting sob began the world. Not this world, O not this! The world that sets this right." (Chapter lxv.)

From *Hard Times:*—

"'Angels are not like me. Between them and a working woman, full of faults, there is a deep gulf set. My little sister is among them, but she is changed.'

". . . 'Thou'rt an angel ; it may be thou hast saved my soul alive. . . . And so I will try t' look t' th' time when thou and me at last shall walk together far awa,' beyond the deep gulf, in th' country where thy little sister is.'" (Book i., chapter xiii.)

"The star had shown him where to find the God of the poor; and through humility, and sorrow, and forgiveness, he had gone to his Redeemer's rest." (Book i., chapter vii.)

From *Little Dorrit:*—

"It would be as hard to convince me that if I were to pass into the other world to-morrow, I should not, through the mercy of God, be received there by a daughter, just like Pet." (Book i., chapter ii.)

"The two brothers were before their Father; far beyond the twilight judgments of this world; high above its mist and obscurities." (Book ii., chapter xix.)

From *A Tale of Two Cities:*—

"The immortal creature that was to be so butchered and torn asunder." (Book ii., chapter i.)

"Even when golden hair, like her own, lay in a halo on a pillow round the worn face of a little boy, and he said, with a radiant smile, 'Dear papa and mamma, I am very sorry to leave you both, and to leave my pretty sister; but I am called, and I must go!' those were not all tears of agony that wetted his young mother's cheek, and the spirit departed from her embrace that had been entrusted to it. Suffer them and forbid them not. They see my Father's face. O Father, blessed words! Thus, the rustling of an angel's wings got blended with the other echoes, and they were not wholly of earth, but had in them the breath of heaven." (Book ii., chapter xxi.)

"We shall meet again, where the weary are at rest." (Book iii., chapter xi.)

From *Our Mutual Friend:*—

"All the light that shone on Betty Highdew lay beyond death."

"Lizzie Hexam very softly raised the weather-stained grey head, and lifted her as high as heaven." (Book iii., chapter viii.)

There is a "beautiful and affecting incident," as he himself terms it, "associated with a shipwreck," recorded in one of his writings, in which a crew are cast ashore on a savage coast. Amongst them is a little child, who is made a sacred charge. "Beset by lions and tigers, by savages, by thirst, by hunger, by death in a crowd of shapes, they never—O Father of all mankind, Thy name be blessed for it!—forget this child." A rough carpenter becomes his special friend, but he dies, and the steward succeeds to the sacred guardianship of the child. "God knows all he does for the poor baby; how he cheerfully carries him in his arms, when he himself is weak and ill; how he feeds him when he himself is griped with want; how he folds his ragged jacket around him, lays his little worn face with a woman's tenderness upon his sunburnt breast, soothes him in his sufferings, sings to him as he limps along, unmindful of his own parched and bleeding feet." And when the child dies—

"His faithful friend, the steward, lingers but a little while behind him. His grief is great, he staggers on for a few days, lies down in the desert, and dies. But he shall be reunited in his immortal spirit—*who can doubt it?*—with the child, when he and the poor carpenter shall be raised up with the words, 'Inasmuch as ye have done it unto the least of these, ye have done it unto Me.'" ("The Long Voyage.")

"A Child's Dream of a Star" might be quoted in its entirety as illustrative. It is a little allegory, written in a childish strain, apparently to inculcate the truth of Immorality. A few extracts will show the tenor of the conception—

". . . They wondered at the goodness of the power of God who made the lovely world . . . And so the time came, all too soon! when the child looked out alone . . . when the star made long rays down towards him, as he saw it through his tears. Now, these rays were so bright, and they seemed to make such a shining ray from earth to heaven, that when the child went to his solitary bed, he dreamed about the star; and dreamed that, lying where he was, he saw a train of people taken up that sparkling road by angels. And the star, opening, showed him a great world of light, where many more such angels waited to receive them. . . . His sister's angel lingered near the entrance of the star, and said to the leader among those who had brought the people thither; 'Is my brother come?' And he said 'No.' She was turning hopefully away, when the child stretched out his arms, and cried 'O, sister, I am here! Take me!' and then she turned her beaming eyes upon him, and it was night; and the star was shining into the room, making long rays down towards him as he saw it through his tears. From that hour forth the child looked out upon the star as on the home he was to go to, when his time should come. . . . There was a baby born to be a brother to the child; and while he was so little that he never yet had spoken word, he stretched his tiny form out on his bed and died. . . . He grew to be a young man, and was busy at his books when an old servant came to him and said, 'Thy mother is no more.' . . . Again at night he saw the star. . . . A mighty cry of joy went forth through all the star, because the mother was reunited to her two children. . . . The man who had been the child saw his daughter, newly lost to him, a celestial creature among those three. . . . Thus the child came to be an old man. . . . They whispered one another, 'He is dying.' And he said, 'I am. My age is falling from me like a garment, and I move towards the star as a child. And O, my Father, now I thank Thee that it has so often opened, to receive those dear ones who await me.'"

With one more pregnant sentence—"The sure and certain hope which Christmas inspired" ("Seven Poor Travellers")—I bring the quotations under this head to a close. Sufficient has been given to define his sentiments on "Immortality," but the patient reader will readily be able to add largely to the list. I pass on to his sentiments upon

GOD.

In the course of the books the Almighty is alluded to under all His attributes—as (1.) Creator, (2.) Father, (3.) Judge.

1. *God the Creator and Disposer.*

From *The Old Curiosity Shop:*—

"I love these little people; and it is not a slight thing that they, who are so fresh from God, love us." (Chapter i.)

"The ties that bind the wealthy and the proud to home may be forged on earth, but those which link the poor man to his humble hearth are of the truer metal, and bear the stamp of heaven. . . . His household gods are of flesh and blood, with no alloy of silver, gold, or precious stone; he has no property but in the affections of his own heart; and when they endear bare floors and walls, despite of rags and toil and scanty fare, that man has his love of home from God, and his rude hut becomes a solemn place." (Chapter xxxviii.)

"Kit's mother can reach his hand through the bars, and she clasps it—God, and those to whom He has given such tenderness, only know in how much agony." (Chapter lxiii.)

"She was wise enough to think that by *a good and merciful dispensation* this must be human nature." (Chapter liii.)

"She seemed a creature fresh from the hand of God, and waiting for the breath of life; not one who had lived and suffered death." (Chapter lxxi.)

From *Barnaby Rudge:*—

"It is something to know that heaven has left the capacity of gladness in such a creature's" (the idiot's) "breast; it is something to be assured that, however lightly men may crush that faculty in their fellows, the Great Creator of mankind imparts it even to his despised and slighted work." (Chapter xxv.)

From the *Battle of Life:*—

". . . A world of sacred mystery, and our Creator only knows what lies under the surface of His lightest image."

From *Little Dorrit:*—

". . . How much, or how little, of the wretched truth it pleased God to make known to her, lies hidden with many mysteries." (Book i., chapter vii.)

From *A Tale of Two Cities:*—

"Dr. Manette speaks of the time when a gracious God restored his faculties." (Book i., chapter iii.)

From *Our Mutual Friend:*—

". . . They have been the truth since the foundations of the universe were laid, and they will be the truth until the foundations of the universe are shaken by the Builder." (Book iii., chapter viii.)

From the *Child's History of England:*—

"It is not the sea alone that is bidden to go 'Thus far, and no farther.' The great command goes forth to all the kings upon the earth, and went to Canute in the year 1035, and stretched him dead upon his bed." (Chapter v.)

2. *The Fatherhood and Mercy of God.*

From *American Notes:*—

"The spiritual and affectionate friendships existing amongst the blind is a part of the great scheme of heaven's merciful consideration for the afflicted." (Chapter iii.)

From *Dombey and Son:*—

". . . That higher Father, who does not reject his children's love." (Chapter xiii.)

From *David Copperfield:*—

"I know that, but for the mercy of God, I might have easily been, for any care that was taken of me, a little robber or a little vagabond." (Chapter xi.)

From *Little Dorrit:*—

"Mrs. Meagles, at the Foundling Hospital, says, 'O dear, dear! when I saw all those children ranged tier above tier, and appealing from the father none of them had ever known upon earth, to the great Father of us all in heaven. . . .'" (Book i., chapter ii.)

"The two brothers were before their Father." (Book ii., chapter xx.)

From the *Seven Poor Travellers :—*

"The Divine Forgiver of injuries."

From *The Haunted Man :—*

"Oh, Father, so much better than earthly fathers, take this wanderer back."

Faith in God appropriately ranges itself under this heading, and as prayer is essentially the outcome of that faith, I shall here take the opportunity of summing up the strong expressions of Charles Dickens's confidence in the goodness and mercy of the Almighty, so far as they bear upon the subject now in hand, and shall show that. prayer was no formal or perfunctory Christian adjunct with him, but a real, vitalising power, and a further evidence of the reality of his Christian character.

There are many praying characters in his books, whose sincerity is sufficiently evidenced to guarantee us in accepting their faith as the reflection of his own. Indeed, nearly all the best types of elevated and pure character delineated by him are praying people, and this very coincidence is expressive enough, as an essential in his ideal of such character. Readers of his writings will corroborate this in perusing the following references :—

In the *Pickwick Papers*, the mother of the clergyman's story fervently beseeches the Almighty Being who had hitherto supported her in all her trouble, to release her from a world of woe and misery, and to spare the life of her only child. The prayer is answered, in that, though her heart is breaking, no complaint or murmur escapes her lips from that time, and, after her death, her prodigal and convict son becomes truly contrite, penitent, and humbled. (Chapter vi.) It somewhat detracts, by-the-by, from the influence of this story, that Mr. Pickwick, immediately afterwards, is shown to his comfortable bedroom, and in less than five minutes after that falls sound asleep, evidently without saying *his* prayers, and that this fact is referred to the "somniferous influence of the clergyman's story."

In *Oliver Twist* Mrs. Maylie, Rose, and Oliver pray; and poor degraded Nancy learns from Rose that faith which enables her to breathe to her Maker one prayer for mercy in her dying moments.

In *Nicholas Nickleby* Godfrey Nickleby commends his wife and children to God, and Smike is alluded to, more than once, as in the act of prayer. In his dying moments he is shown to be in much communion with heaven. The Cheeryble Brothers render occasional momentary homage to God.

The beautiful conception of Little Nell is greatly dependent for its claim to our admiration in her elevated spirituality and dependence on God. Ere leaving her home for her wanderings, she looks upon the little room where she had so often knelt down and prayed at nights (chapter xii.); she prays that God would raise up some friend for her grandfather, while she has no thoughts for any wants of her own (chapter xlv.); she thinks that if she lives to reach the open country again, though it be only to lay down and die, with what a grateful heart she will thank God for so much mercy (*ibid*); she promises the boy she will remain on earth as long as heaven will let her (chapter lv.); and she dies the calm and happy death of a Christian. Her old grandfather prays, too, that she might come again to-morrow, but his imbecility or dotage debars that being offered as evidence. But the supposed narrator of the story, old Humphrey, speaks in a spirit of Christian dependence, and of him it is said, that after death, "his face wore a serene, benign expression, with something in it so very spiritual, so strangely and indefinably allied to youth, although his head was grey and venerable, that it was new even in him."

The widow Rudge, a Roman Catholic, is depicted as a woman of strong prayerful instincts. Here is a prayer from her lips:—

"Oh Thou who hast taught me such deep love for this one remnant of the promise of a happy life, out of whose affliction even, perhaps, the comfort springs that he is ever a relying, loving child to me—never growing old or cold at heart, but needing my care and duty in his manly strength as in his cradle-time—help him, in his darkened walk through this sad world, or he is doomed, and my poor heart is broken." (*Barnaby Rudge*, chapter xvii.)

Her strong reliance on God is forcibly depicted in her interview with Mr. Haredale, in chapter xxv.; and in her interview with her guilty husband in the prison she thus urges repentance and religion upon him :—

"Listen to me for one moment. . . . I am but newly-risen from a sick-bed, from which I never hoped to rise again. The best among us think, at such a time, of good intentions half performed and duties left undone. If I have ever, since that fatal night, omitted to pray for your repentance before death—if I omitted, even then, anything which might tend to urge it on you when the horror of your crime was fresh—if, in our later meeting, I yielded to the dread that was upon me, and forgot to fall upon my knees and solemnly adjure you, in the name of him you sent to his account with heaven, to prepare for the retribution which must come, and which is stealing on you now—I humbly before you, and in the agony of supplication in which you see me, beseech that you will let me make atonement. . . . Husband, dear husband, if you will but confess this dreadful crime; if you will but implore forgiveness of heaven, and of those whom you have wronged on earth; if you will dismiss these vain, uneasy thoughts, which never can be realised, and will rely on penitence and on the truth, I promise you, in the great name of the Creator, whose image you have defaced, that He will comfort and console you. As for myself, I swear before Him, as He knows my heart and reads it now, that from that hour I will love and cherish you as I did of old, and watch you night and day in the short interval that will remain to us, and soothe you with my truest love and duty, and pray with you, that one threatening judgment may be arrested, and that our boy may be spared to bless God, in his poor way, in the free air and light." (Chapter lxxiii.)

In *Martin Chuzzlewit* Ruth Pinch breathes John Westlock's name upon her knees, and pours out her pure heart before that Being from whom such hearts and such affections come. (Chapter liv.)

In *Dombey and Son* faithful, noble-hearted Florence prays to God to let one angel (her brother's) love her and remember her (chapter xviii.); again, she prays in her mind to God to bless her father, and to soften him towards her, if it might be so; and if not, to forgive him if he was wrong, and pardon her the prayer which almost seemed impiety (book ii., chapter xiii.); and again, when she only knew that she had no father upon earth, she said so, many times, with her suppliant head hidden from all but her Father who was in heaven (book ii., chapter xix.).

David Copperfield prays that he may not forget the houseless (chapter xiii.); and of that good and faithful servant, Peggotty, his childish heart is certain that the Lord will one day say, "Well done." In the same book many expressions might be culled from the sayings of Daniel Peggotty, showing a steadfast reliance on the Almighty, the most expressive of which is his thanksgiving on his erring niece's restoration to him :—

"Mas'r Davy, I thank my Heav'nly Father as my dream's come true! I thank Him hearty for having guided me, in His own ways, to my darling." (Chapter li.)

Inseparable from David Copperfield, too, is Agnes, with her face "so full of pity and of grief, that rain of tears, that awful mute appeal to me, that solemn hand upraised towards heaven!"—telling of Dora's death. (Chapter lv.) And then, at length, together, David and Agnes thank their God, as they look up at the stars, for having guided them to their tranquillity in the knowledge of each other's love. (Chapter lxiii.)

In *Bleak House* Esther prays in all her emergencies, and is spoken of as pouring out her heart for herself and for her unhappy mother. (Chapter xxxvi.)

In *A Tale of Two Cities* Lucy Darnay, on her husband's salvation from the guillotine, says, "Oh, dearest Charles, let me thank God for this on my knees as I have prayed to Him," whereupon they all reverently bowed their heads and hearts. (Book iii., chapter vi.) Charles Darnay, when again doomed to die, relies on God to raise up friends for his wife, while she professes to have strength given her to bear the separation. (Book iii., chapter xi.) Awaiting death, he is devoutly thankful to heaven for his recovered self-possession. (Chapter xiii.) Dr. Manette speaks of a gracious God restoring his faculties (book i., chapter iii.); and Mr. Lorry thanks heaven that none dear to him are in Paris during the awful scenes he is a witness of (book ii., chapter iii.)

In *Our Mutual Friend* Betty Higden relies upon God in preference to the Poor-law Board; and coming to the end of her weary pilgrimage, she holds up her withered hands, and thanks the Power and the Glory that she has come to her journey's end, and sinking at the foot of a tree, she thinks of the Cross, and commits herself to Him who died upon it. (Book iii., chapter viii.) The Boffins are described as having guided themselves so far on the journey of life by a religious sense of duty and desire to do right. (Book i., chapter ix.) And, what is very much to our purpose, there are two prayers recorded in which Lizzie Hexam beseeches strength to rescue Eugene from the river after Bradley Headstone's murderous attack upon him :—

"Now, merciful heaven be thanked for that old time, and grant, O Blessed Lord, that through Thy wonderful workings it may turn to good at last! To whomsoever the drifting face belongs, be it man's or woman's, help my humble hands, Lord God, to raise it from death and restore it to some one to whom it must be dear."

. . . .

"Now, merciful heaven be thanked for that old time, enabling me, without a wasted moment, to have got the boat afloat again, and to row back against the stream! And grant, O Blessed Lord God, that through poor me he may be raised from death, and preserved to some one else to whom he may be dear one day, though never dearer than to me!" (Book iv., chapter vii.)

There is a realisation here of something more than mere prayerful reliance; there is an acknowledgment of God's overruling providence, of His moving in mysterious ways, His wondrous works to do, and a recognition of the great assurance that "all things work together for good to those who love God."

In *Great Expectations* Pip knows of no better words to say to the dying Magwitch than "O Lord be merciful to him a sinner," (chapter lvi.); and again, after being nursed in his illness by Joe, he penitently whispers, "O God, bless him! God bless this gentle Christian man!"

"The Wreck of the Golden Mary" is full of prayerful feeling from beginning to end. Captain Ravender knows that his mother never lays down her head at night without having said, "Merciful Lord! bless and preserve William George Ravender, and send him straight home, through Jesus Christ our Saviour!" "We'll all stand by one another ashore, yet, please God, my lads!" says he, when they put off in the long-boat; and seeing the ship go down from there, he says, "Let every one here thank the Lord for our preservation!" All the voices answered, "We thank the Lord!" Then the captain said the Lord's Prayer. The burial of the child is a beautiful and pathetic piece of reading :—

"It troubled me all night to think that there was no prayer-book among us, and that I could remember but very few of the exact words of the burial service. When I stood up at broad day, all knew what was going to be done, and I noticed that my poor fellows made the motion of uncovering their heads, though their heads had been stark bare to the sky and sea for many a weary hour. There was a long heavy swell on, but otherwise it was a fair morning, and there were broad fields of sunlight on the waves in the east. I said no more than this: 'I am the Resurrection and the Life, saith the Lord. He raised the daughter of Jairus the ruler, and said she was not dead but slept. He raised the widow's son. He arose Himself, and was seen of many. He loved little children, saying, Suffer them to come unto Me and rebuke them not, for of such is the kingdom of heaven. In His name, my friends, and committed to His merciful goodness!' With these words I laid my rough face softly on the placid little forehead, and buried the Golden Lucy in the grave of the Golden Mary."

That faith was an essential principle in Dickens's religion, and ranked in his mind far above creeds and dogmas, is obvious by the following quotations, selected from many similar :—

"Betty Higden . . . was . . . not a logically-reasoning woman, but God is good, and hearts may count in heaven as high as heads." (*Our Mutual Friend*, book i., chapter xv.)

When Barnaby Rudge, in prison, parts from his mother—

"The moon came up in all her gentle glory, and the stars looked out, and through the small compass of the grated window, as through the narrow crevice of one good deed in a mirky life of guilt, the face of heaven shone bright and merciful. He raised his head; gazed upward at the quiet sky, which seemed to smile upon the earth in sadness, as if the night,

more thoughtful than the day, looked down in sorrow on the
sufferings and evil deeds of men ; and felt its peace sink deep
into his heart. He, a poor idiot, caged in his narrow cell, was
as much lifted up to God, while gazing on the mild light, as the
freest and most favoured man in all the spacious city ; and in
his ill-remembered prayer, and in the fragment of the childish
hymn with which he sung and crooned himself asleep, there
breathed as true a spirit as ever studied homily expressed, or
old cathedral arches echoed." (Chapter lxiii.)

And the quotation from a *Child's History of England*,
already adduced, in connection with excommunication :—

"This unchristian nonsense would, of course, have made no
difference to the person cursed—who could say his prayers at
home if he were shut out of church, and whom none but
God could judge." (Chapter xii.)

An article of his faith, associated with the Fatherhood
of God, more than once made prominent in his writings, is
observable in the following quotations :—

Captain Ravender tells the shipwrecked party that—

"Nothing vanished from the eye of God, though much might
pass away from the eyes of men. 'We were all of us,' says I,
'children once ; and our baby feet have strolled in green woods
ashore ; and our baby hands have gathered flowers in gardens,
where the birds were singing. The children that we were are
not lost to the great knowledge of our Creator. Those innocent
creatures will appear with us before Him, and plead for us.
What we were in the best time of our generous youth will arise
and go with us too. The purest part of our lives will not desert
us at the pass to which all of us here present are gliding.
What we were then will be as much in existence before Him as
what we are now." ("The Wreck of the Golden Mary.")

Old Philip Swidger, in the *Haunted Man*, also gives
expression to this curious idea, when he stands by the bed
of his dying prodigal son :—

"I was thankful, only yesterday, that I could remember this

unhappy son when he was an innocent child. But what a comfort it is now to think that even God Himself has that remembrance of him.

"Oh, Father, so much better than the fathers upon earth! Oh, Father! so much more afflicted by the errors of Thy children, take this wanderer back. Not as he is, but as he was then, let him cry unto Thee, as he has so often seemed to cry to us."

At so early a stage of his experience as *Oliver Twist* we read an allusion to this same article of belief, in these words :—

"It is a common thing for the countenances of the dead, even in that fixed and rigid state, to subside into the long-forgotten expression of sleeping infancy, and settle into the very look of early life; so calm, so peaceful, do they grow again, that those who knew them in their happy childhood, kneel by the coffin's side in awe, and see the angel even upon earth." (Chapter xxiv.)

3. *God our Judge.*

While he relies upon the great and fatherly goodness of "that Being whose code is mercy" (*Oliver Twist*, chapter liii.), he does not presume upon that mercy to escape the fact that God is also our judge, and that we are responsible to Him; and he clearly apprehends the retribution that inevitably overtakes the wicked, and the terrors that appal their guilty, awakened consciences.

Rudge, the murderer, is spoken of as being the visible object of the Almighty's wrath (chapter lxv.); and the description of his conscience, appalled by the sound of the alarm-bell, reminding him of the time when it rang out the news of the discovery of his crime, is one of the most vivid and terrible realisations that has perhaps ever been penned :—

"It was not the sudden change from darkness to this dreadful light, it was was not the sound of distant shrieks and shouts of triumph, it was not this dread invasion of the serenity and peace of night, that drove the man back as though a thunderbolt had struck him. It was the Bell! If the ghastliest shape the human mind has ever pictured in its wildest dreams had risen up before him, he could not have staggered backward from his touch as he did from the first sound of that loud iron voice. With eyes that started from his head, his limbs convulsed, his face most horrible to see, he raised one arm high up into the air, and holding something visionary back and down, with his other hand drove at it as though he held a knife and stabbed it to the heart. He clutched his hair, and stopped his ears, and travelled madly round and round; then gave a frightful cry, and with it rushed away; still, still, the bell tolled on and seemed to follow him—louder and louder, hotter and hotter yet. The glare grew brighter, the roar of voices deeper; the crash of heavy bodies falling, shook the air; bright streams of sparks rose up into the sky; but louder than them all—rising, faster far, to heaven—a million times more fierce and furious—pouring forth dreadful secrets after its long silence—speaking the language of the dead—the Bell—the Bell!

"What haunt of spectres could surpass that dread pursuit and flight! Had there been a legion of them on his track he could better have borne it. They would have had a beginning and an end, but here all space was full. The one pursuing voice was everywhere: it sounded in the earth, the air; shook the long grass, and howled among the trembling trees. The echoes caught it up, the owls hooted as it flew upon the breeze, the nightingale was silent and hid herself among the thickest boughs; it seemed to goad and urge the angry fire, and lash it into madness; everything was steeped in the one prevailing red; the glow was everywhere; nature was drenched in blood: still the remorseless crying of that awful voice—the Bell, the Bell!

"It ceased; but not in his ears. The knell was at his heart. No work of man had ever voice like that which sounded there, and warned him that it cried unceasingly to heaven. Who could hear that bell, and not know what it said? There was murder in its every note—cruel, relentless, savage murder—the murder of a confiding man, by one who held his every trust. Its ringing summoned phantoms from their graves. What face was that, in which a friendly smile changed to a look of half incredulous horror, which stiffened for a moment into one of pain, then changed into an imploring glance at heaven, and so fell idly down with upturned eyes, like the dead stag's he had so often peeped at when a little child : shrinking and shuddering—there was a dreadful thing to think of now !—and clinging to an apron as he looked ! He sank upon the ground, and grovelling down as if he would dig himself a place to hide in, covered his face and ears ; but no, no, no—a hundred walls and roofs of brass would not shut out the bell, *for in it spoke the wrathful voice of God, and from that voice the whole wide universe could not afford a refuge.*" (Chapter lv.)

In three other notable instances the same warning is forcibly given—warnings that no guilty conscience could possibly read unmoved ; and who can say what hardened hearts they may have pierced before to-day, and how far they may have contributed to that conviction which is the infallible precusor to the salvation of sinners !

In "The Drunkard's Death" (*Sketches by Boz*), one of these instances occurs :—

" It is a dreadful thing to wait and watch for the approach of death ; to know that hope is gone, and recovery impossible ; and to sit and count the dreary hours through long, long nights —such nights as only watchers by the bed of sickness know. It chills the blood to hear the dearest secrets of the heart—the pent-up, hidden secrets of many years—poured forth by the unconscious helpless being before you ; and to think how little the reserve and cunning of a whole life will avail, when fever and delirium tear off the mask at last. Strange tales have been told in the wanderings of dying men ; tales so full of guilt and crime, that those who stood by have fled in horror and affright, lest they should be scared to madness by what they heard and saw; and many a wretch has died alone, raving of deeds the very name of which has driven the boldest man away."

Sikes, after the murder of Nancy, and Jonas Chuzzlewit, after the murder of Montague, are the two other examples alluded to. In describing the horror with which the conscience of the former is infected, this moral is drawn:—

"Let no man talk of murderers escaping justice, and hint that Providence must sleep. There were twenty score of violent deaths in one long minute of that agony of fear." (*Oliver Twist*, chapter xlviii.)

The mental agonies of Jonas Chuzzlewit, his horror of the crime, his continual dread of the certainty of its discovery, always accompanied with a sense of triumph at the removal of the obstacle who had been his evil genius, and without a gleam of repentance in the murky blackness of his soul, is a powerful delineation of retributive justice. And, as a text to this early formed article of his religion, may be cited a passage in *Oliver Twist*:—

"Oh! if, when we oppress and grind our fellow-creatures, we bestowed but one thought on the dark evidences of human error, which, like dense and heavy clouds, are rising, slowly it is true, but not less surely, to heaven, to pour their after-vengeance on our heads; if we heard but one instant, in imagination, the deep testimony of dead men's voices, which no power can stifle, and no pride shut out; where would be the injury and injustice, the suffering, misery, cruelty, and wrong, that each day's life brings with it!" (Chapter xxx.)

While these passages speak of retributive justice in this life, his appreciation of the doctrine of the judgment in the future state is no less forcibly expressed in many passages, and the right of judgment deferred to the Almighty. His views on this great matter will be seen to be in strict accordance with the teachings of the Bible:—

"The sun was striking in at the great windows of the court, through the glittering drops of rain upon the glass, and it made a broad shaft of light between the two-and-thirty and the judge, linking both together, and perhaps reminding some among the audience how both were passing on, with absolute equality, to the greater judgment that knoweth all things and cannot err." (*Great Expectations*, chapter lvi.)

" Yes, Steerforth, long removed from the scenes of this poor history! My sorrow may bear involuntary witness against you at the judgment-throne ; but my angry thoughts or my reproaches never will, I know!" (*David Copperfield*, chapter xlviii.)

David Copperfield says to Martha, when she hints at the river as an end for her miseries :—

" In the name of the Great Judge, before whom you and all of us must stand at His dread time, dismiss that terrible idea." (Chapter xlvii.)

In the account of the taking of the Bastile, in *A Tale of Two Cities*, seven dead prisoners are spoken of as being carried out of the prison, whose drooping eyelids and half-seen eyes awaited the Last Day :—

" Impassive faces, yet with a suspended—not an abolished—expression on them ; faces, rather, in a fearful pause, as having yet to raise the dropped lids of the eyes, and bear witness with the bloodless lips, 'THOU DID'ST IT!'" (Chapter xxi.)

In the *Child's History of England* Gardiner is spoken of as having gone to his tremendous account before God ; and it is written that " they threw Joan's ashes into the river Seine; but they will rise against her murderers on the last day."

The following passages agree with the scripture teaching of the relegation of this judgment to a definite day—the Day of Judgment :—

" Oh, woman, God beloved in old Jerusalem! The best among us need deal lightly with thy faults, if only for the punishment thy nature will endure, in bearing heavy evidence against us on the day of judgment !" (*Martin Chuzzlewit*, chapter xxix.)

" Slavery . . . the dangers to society with which it is

fraught: dangers which . . . are as certain to fall upon its guilty head as is the Day of Judgment." (*American Notes*, chapter xvii.)

"What if the prisoner now sleeping quietly . . . by the light of the Great Day of Judgment should trace back his fall to her." (*Little Dorrit*, chapter viii.)

The acknowledgment of the Day of Judgment necessitates the acceptance of the doctrine of the Resurrection, and this we find assented to in the remarkably expressive type of that mystery, detailed in *The Chimes*:—

"Black are the brooding clouds and troubled the deep waters, when the Sea of Thought, first heaving from a calm, gives up its dead. Monsters uncouth and wild arise in premature, imperfect resurrection; the several shapes and parts of different things are joined and mixed by chance; and when, and how, and by what wonderful degrees, each separate from each, and every sense and object of the mind resumes its usual form and lives again, no man—though every man is every day the casket of this type of the great mystery—can tell."

In the visit to the scene of the wreck of the *Royal Charter*, and the home of the clergyman so honourably associated with that event in the *Uncommercial Traveller*, the churchyard is called the type of death, and the clergyman's dwelling side by side with it the type of resurrection.

Noteworthy, as being one of the last sentences he penned in his last book, is the following:—

"A brilliant morning shines on the old city . . . changes of glorious light from moving boughs, songs of birds, scents from gardens, woods, and fields—or, rather, from the one great garden of the whole cultivated island in its yielding time—penetrate into the cathedral, subdue its earthly odour, and preach the resurrection and the life." (*Edwin Drood*, chapter xxiii.)

CHAPTER VII.

Charles Dickens on Christian Doctrine—(continued)

THE ATONEMENT AND PERSON OF CHRIST.

HE reliance of Charles Dickens on this great and central doctrine of Christianity is at once definitely established by the words of his own will, and would render further evidence unnecessary, but for the plan and scope marked out in the compilation of this volume. The evidence to be collected under this head will be well prefaced by the declaration of his matured and defined profession of faith, made at that solemn period when he was putting in order his affairs in this world, and, of necessity, being reminded that here he had no abiding city. The words relative to our subject are very conclusive, and an index to the views he ever consistently adhered to, and a summary of his religious sentiments :—

" I commit my soul to the mercy of God through our Lord and Saviour Jesus Christ, and I exhort my dear children humbly to try and guide themselves by the teaching of the New Testament in its broad spirit, and to put no faith in any man's narrow construction of its letter here or there."

In none of his first five books—from The *Sketches* to

Barnaby Rudge inclusive—do I find anything that I can construe into a Confession of Faith in the world's Redeemer. We have seen, from the very first, that he, judging by the sentiments he wrote in his books, acknowledged the sovereignty, fatherhood, and goodness of God, the immortality of the soul, and the efficacy of prayer; but whatever progress the growth of his finally-established religious convictions may have been during that period, he committed himself to no allusion to that all-important theme until he penned the *American Notes*, which followed *Barnaby Rudge*. Here one passage only alludes to Jesus Christ—not as Saviour, however—but simply in words that no honest investigator could grudge to the spotless and holy character of the Messiah, even though he held Him to be no more than a man of God:—

"Let that poor hand of hers (Laura Bridgman, the blind mute) lie gently on your hearts; for there may be something in its healing touch akin to that of the Great Master whose precepts you misconstrue, whose lessons you pervert, of whose charity and sympathy with all the world not one among you in his daily practice knows as much as many of the worst among those fallen sinners to whom you are liberal in nothing but the preachment of perdition." (Chapter iii.)

There is, it will be confessed, nothing more here than the tribute that even a Socinian might render to Jesus Christ, if not, indeed, a suggestion that the influence might be resolved into the mere human effect that sympathy and chastened suffering has upon impressible natures. Be this as it may, it is very curious to learn, from his biographer, John Foster, that at this very time he had sittings in the Little Portland Street Unitarian Chapel, which step he took in his impatience of differences with clergymen of the Established Church, but that he returned to his original communion at the lapse of two or three years, and remained a consistent member of it until his death. In the same connection, as elsewhere in the memoirs, allusion is made to the frequent agitation of his mind and thoughts in connection with this all-important theme. It is noteworthy that no allusion is made to Christ or the Atonement in the book written during this period of indecision, and it is not until the publication of the Christmas book of the *Chuzzlewit* year—at which period, I conclude, his connection was severed with the Unitarians—that we find a more decided tone used in alluding to this doctrine. It may be a very beautiful description of the light breaking in upon his own darkness when he writes :—

"Why did I walk through crowds of fellow-beings, with my eyes turned down, and never raise them to that blessed Star which led the wise men to a poor abode?" (*Christmas Carol.*)

This book called forth the highest commendations. Thackeray called it "a national benefit," and Jeffrey congratulated him on having, by its publication, fostered more kindly feeling, and prompted more positive acts of beneficence, than can be traced to all the pulpits and confessionals in Christendom since Christmas 1842 (the Carol was published Christmas 1843). Only once again, however, is the Redeemer alluded to, where the words "And He took a little child, and set him in the midst," are quoted as the solace which Bob Cratchit finds for the loss of Tiny Tim.

Between this and the next book—*The Chimes*—he records, in a letter written to John Foster, a curious dream he had, in which he saw the departed spirit of one who was dear to him, and which he asked, in an agony of entreaty, "What is the true religion?"

"As it paused," he continued, "a moment without replying, I said—Good God, in such an agony of haste, lest it should go away!—'You think, as I do, that the form of religion does not so greatly matter, if we try to do good? or,' I said, observing that it still hesitated and was moved with the greatest compassion for me, 'perhaps the Roman Catholic is the best? perhaps it makes one think of God oftener, and believe in Him more steadily?' 'For *you*,' said the spirit, full of such heavenly tenderness for me, that I felt as if my heart would break; 'for *you*, it is the best!'"

This would seem to evidence the unsettled state of his mind upon religion at this period. He speaks, at the close of the letter, of being uncertain whether to look upon the dream as a dream only, or as an actual vision. But that he did not remain long in doubt as to the relative virtues of the Roman Catholic and Protestant faiths is evidenced by those sentiments upon the former already adduced. The letter was written from Italy, and the very fact of his residence there during this crisis in his religious history may have had great influence upon his ultimate decision. That what he saw there of the national faith impressed him very unfavourably, the *Pictures from Italy* shows; and not the least forcible comment upon it is that keen satire upon the system which was responsible for the iniquities of the Inquisition, in which he satirically terms the administrators of its fiendish tortures, "His chosen servants, true believers in the Sermon on the Mount, elect disciples of Him who never did a miracle but to heal; who never struck a man with palsy, blindness, deafness, dumbness, madness, any one affliction of mankind; and never stretched His blessed hand out but to give relief and ease!"

From this time there is neither reservation nor hesitation in his allusions to Jesus Christ, which flow naturally and unobtrusively from his pen, and are everywhere characterised by a reverential modesty which speaks well for the soundness of his now decided faith, as there are good grounds so to term it from this time forward.

In the Christmas book of that year there are two instances:—

"He suffered her to sit beside His feet, and to dry them with her hair."

. . . . . .

"The officer appointed to dispense the public charity (the lawful charity; not that once preached upon a mount.)" (*The Chimes.*)

Dombey and Son, which, excepting for the intermediate Christmas book, the *Cricket on the Hearth*, is the next book, chronologically, supplies the next item of evidence:—

"Harriet complied and read—read the eternal book for all the weary and the heavy-laden; for all the wretched, fallen, and neglected of this earth—read the blessed history, in which the blind, lame, palsied beggar, the criminal, the woman stained with shame, the shunned of all our dainty clay, has each a portion, that no human pride, indifference, or sophistry, through all the ages that this world shall last, can take away, or by the thousandth atom of a grain reduce—read the ministry of Him who, through the round of human life, and all its hopes and griefs, from birth to death, from infancy to age, had sweet compassion for, and interest in its every scene and stage, its every suffering and sorrow.

"'I shall come,' said Harriet, when she shut the book, 'very early in the morning.'

"The lustrous eyes, yet fixed upon her face, closed for a moment, then opened; and Alice kissed and blest her.

"The same eyes followed her to the door; and in their light, and on the tranquil face, there was a smile when it was closed.

"They never turned away. She laid her hand upon her breast, murmuring the sacred name that had been read to her; and life passed from her face, like light removed." (Chapter lvii.)

In that curious and beautiful tale, *The Haunted Man*, which is based upon an article of Christian faith, and teems with religious sentiment, we meet with two examples of confidence in the Atonement:—

(1.) Redlaw's prayer :—"Oh Thou, who, through the teaching of pure love, has graciously restored me to the memory which was once the memory of Christ upon the Cross, and of all the good who have perished in His cause, receive my thanks."

(2.) "Then, as Christmas is a time in which, of all times in the year, the memory of every remediable sorrow, wrong, and trouble in the world around us, should be active with us, not less than our own experience, for all good, he laid his hand upon the boy, and silently calling Him to witness who laid His hand on children in old time, rebuking, in the majesty of His prophetic knowledge, those who kept them from Him, vowed to protect him, teach him, and reclaim him."

In *David Copperfield* Mrs. Gummidge comforts Dan'l Peggotty with Christ's promise, "As you have done it unto one of the least of these, you have done it unto Me" (chapter xxxii.); and in *Bleak House*, Esther and Ada whisper to the bereaved mother what Our Saviour said of children (chapter viii.). In the *Child's History of England*, chapter vi. concludes with the words, "You know, however, who really touched the sick, and healed them ; and you know His sacred name is not among the dusty line of human kings ;" and in chapter xxxvi. we note, *en passant*, an allusion to *Our* Saviour's cross.

Hard Times yields three extracts under this head :—

(1.) "Thou knowest who said, ' Let him who is without sin among you cast the first stone at her!'" (Book i., chapter xiii.).

(2.) ". . . Else wherefore live we in a Christian land, eighteen hundred and odd years after our Master?" (Book i., chapter xiv.)

(3.) "The dying Stephen, looking upwards at the star, says to Rachel, 'Often as I come to myself, and found it shinin' on me down there in my trouble, I thowt it were the star as guided to Our Saviour's home. . . . '"

". . . The star had shown him where to find the God of the

poor ; and through humility, and sorrow, and forgiveness, he had gone to his Redeemer's rest." (Book iii., chapter vii.)

In the *Household Words* Christmas story for 1854—"Seven Poor Travellers"—there are several graceful allusions to the Saviour embodied with the text. The giver of the feast to the travellers gives the toast, " Christmas-eve, my friends, when the shepherds, who were poor travellers, too, in their way, heard the angels sing, ' On earth peace, goodwill towards men.' " (Chapter i.) In the story of Richard Doubledick, which forms chapter ii. of the book, occur the words, " In the sweet, compassionate words that naturally present themselves to the mind to-night, ' he was the only son of his mother, and she was a widow.' " Chapter iii. contains a long paragraph much to our purpose :—

" Going through the woods, the softness of my tread upon the mossy ground and among the brown leaves enhanced the Christmas sacredness by which I felt surrounded. As the whitened stems environed me, I thought how the founder of the time had never raised His benignant hand, save to bless and heal, except in the case of one unconscious tree. By Cobham Hall, I came to the village and the churchyard where the dead had been quietly buried, ' in the sure and certain hope ' which Christmas time inspired. What children could I see at play, and not be loving of, recalling who had loved them ! No garden that I passed was out of unison with the day, for I remembered that the tomb was in a garden, and that ' she, supposing Him to be the gardener,' had said, ' Sir, if thou have borne Him hence, tell me where thou hast laid Him, and I will take Him away.' In time, the distant river with the ships came full in view, and with it pictures of the poor fishermen mending their nets, who arose and followed Him—of the teaching of the people from a ship pushed off a little way from shore, by reason of the multitude—of a majestic figure walking on the water in the loneliness of night. My very shadow on the ground was eloquent of Christmas ; for did not the people lay their sick where the mere shadows of the men who had heard and seen Him might fall as they passed along ? "

In *Little Dorrit* there is the eulogy of the gospel of Christ with which the heroine condemns the hard creed of Mrs. Clennam, quoted in chapter v., and one allusion to *Our* Saviour in the last chapter.

In the "Wreck of the Golden Mary" there is the prayer in which Mrs. Ravender commends her son to the mercy of God, "through Christ our Saviour," and the reminiscence of the burial service with which the captain commits the child's body to the sea: "I am the Resurrection and the Life," etc. (*Vide* chapter vii.—on Prayer.)

The *Tale of Two Cities* is prolific in this sentiment. Of Lucie's child it is said, that "the Divine Friend of children, to whom in her trouble she had confided hers, seemed to take her child in His arms, as He took the child of old, and made it a sacred joy to her." (Book ii., chapter xxi.) Sydney Carton, moving towards his voluntary sacrifice, recalls the words he heard at his father's grave, "I am the Resurrection and the Life, saith the Lord: he that believeth on Me, though he were dead, yet shall he live: and whosoever liveth and believeth in Me, shall never die." (Book iii., chapter ix.) Twice on the same page, and yet once again, at the consummation of the sacrifice, are the comforting words repeated; and to the last is superadded that it was said of him, that his was the peacefullest man's face ever beheld there.

In the *Uncommercial Traveller* he rebukes a certain Christian friend "in a beautiful garment," through whose vanity and folly the paupers at St. George's-in-the-East Workhouse had a choir of singing boys to sing for them, and much as they would have liked to, were themselves hindered thereby from singing; upon which he thinks he has read that once the multitude sung for themselves, and that "when they had sung an hymn," some one (not in a beautiful garment) went up into the Mount of Olives. (Chapter iii.)

In the same volume the record of the preaching at the theatre is thus brought to a peroration :—

"In the New Testament there is the most beautiful and affecting history conceivable by man, and there are the terse models for all prayers and for all preaching. As to the models, imitate them, Sunday preachers—else why are they there, consider? As to the history, tell it. Some people cannot read, some people will not read, many people (this especially holds among the young ignorant) find it hard to pursue the verse-form in which the book is presented to them, and imagine that those breaks imply gaps and want of continuity. Help them over that first stumbling-block, by setting forth the history in narrative with no fear of exhausting it. You will never preach so well, you will never move them so profoundly, you will never send them away with half so much to think of. Which is the better interest? Christ's choice of twelve poor men to help in those merciful wonders among the poor and rejected; or the pious bullying of a whole union-full of paupers? What is your changed philosopher to wretched me, peeping in at the door out of the mud of the streets and of my life, when you have the widow's son to tell me about, the ruler's daughter, the other figure at the door when the brother of the two sisters was dead, some of the two ran to the mourner, crying, "The Master is come and calleth for thee?' Let the preacher who will thoroughly forget himself, remember no individuality but one, and no eloquence but one, stand up before four thousand men and women at the Britannia Theatre any Sunday night, recounting that narrative to them as fellow-creatures; he shall see a sight!"

In *Our Mutual Friend* Betty Higden commits her soul to Him who died upon the Cross (book iii., chapter viii.); and, finally, there is the allusion to the resurrection and the life in the last chapter of *Edwin Drood*.

Acknowledgment of the Atonement, of necessity involves the acceptance of the doctrine of

THE FALL OF MAN.

Just as we might have expected, the recognition of this

is manifested before the period of the supposed crisis in his mind regarding the true religion, for in the *Old Curiosity Shop* we read, "Thank God that the innocent joys of others can strongly move us, and that we, even *in our fallen nature,* have one source of pure emotion which must be prized in heaven!" (Chapter xxxii.)

Again, in *Barnaby Rudge,* speaking of the power we have of finding some germs of comfort in the hardest trials, he calls that a redeeming quality which, *even in our fallen nature,* we possess in common with the angels. (Chapter xlvii.)

The expression, "children of the dust," is used in *Bleak House* (chapter xxvii.), and "children of Adam," in *Hard Times* (book ii., chapter ix.).

In the latter book, Rachel (the portraiture of a noble-minded, good woman) says of herself, "Angels are not like me. Between them and a working woman, fu' of faults, there is a deep gulf set. My little sister is among them, *but she is changed.*"* (Book i., chapter xiii.)

Under this head may be cited the Phantom's reproof of Scrooge, in the *Christmas Carol:*—

"Oh, captive-bound and double ironed; not to know that ages of incessant labour, by immortal creatures, for this earth, must pass into eternity before the good of which it is susceptible is all developed. Not to know that any Christian spirit, working kindly in its little sphere, whatever it may be, will

---

* Another extract might be added here, which, with this one, point to a recognition of something very much like the Christian doctrine of Conversion :—

" . . . Never . . . inflict a punishment that cannot be recalled ; while there is a God above us to work changes in the hearts He has made." (*Dombey and Son,* chapter xxxiii.)

The character of Mr. Dombey is well worth studying in this connection, to note the change made in him by his great reverses and by the Christian example and forgiveness of his daughter.

find its mortal life too short for its vast means of usefulness. Not to know that no space of regret can make amends for one life's opportunity missed."

The *Chimes*, too, yields its quota, when, in telling of the wind howling through an empty church at night, the author says—

" . . . It has a ghostly sound, too, lingering within the altar; where it seems to chant, in its wild way, of wrong and murder done, and false gods worshipped, in defiance of the Tables of the Law, which look so fair and smooth, but are so flawed and broken."

"The ruined temple of God," is an expression used in *The Haunted Man*, and is there applied to a fallen woman; and in *A Tale of Two Cities* this scriptural designation is again applied to humanity, when Samson, the executioner ("upon whom the name of the strong man of old scripture had descended"), "tore away the gates of God's own Temple every day." (Book iii., chapter iv.)

Repentance, in connection with the fall of human nature, is endorsed in a sentence in *Dombey and Son*—"Such a look of exultation there may be on angels' faces, when the one repentant sinner enters heaven, among ninety-nine just men." (Chapter lviii.) The doctrine has already been shown to be part of his religious belief, by quotations from earlier books.

PROBATION.

That Charles Dickens recognised the probationary aspect of this life, according to the teachings of scripture, and possessed a thoughtful insight into what has been called the "mystery of suffering," and its sanctifying uses, is evident from many passages in his writings. Indeed, this seems to have been apprehended at an early period of his spiritual history. In the *Old Curiosity Shop* there are two noteworthy passages :—

"The schoolmaster heard her with astonishment. 'This child!'—he thought—'has this child heroically persevered under all doubts and dangers, struggled with poverty and suffering, upheld and sustained by strong affection and the consciousness of rectitude alone! And yet the world is full of such heroism. Have I yet to learn that the hardest and best-borne trials are those which are never chronicled in any earthly record, and are suffered every day!...'" (Chapter xlvi.)

. . . .

"Oh! it is hard to take to heart the lesson that such deaths will teach, but let no man reject it, for it is one that all must learn, and is a mighty, universal truth. When Death strikes down the innocent and young, for every fragile form from which he lets the panting spirit free, a hundred virtues rise, in shapes of mercy, charity, and love, to walk the world and bless it. Of every tear that sorrowing mortals shed on such green graves, some good is born, some gentler nature comes. In the Destroyer's steps there spring up bright creations that defy his power, and his dark path becomes a way of light to heaven." (Chapter lxxii.)

In *Barnaby Rudge* the comfort that the widow experiences in the cheerfulness and affection of her son, idiot though he is; calling to her mind that but for her he might have been sullen, morose, unkind, far removed from her—vicious, perhaps, and cruel!—gives occasion for the sentiment, that, "in the exhaustless catalogue of heaven's mercies to mankind, the power we have of finding some germs of comfort in the hardest trials must ever occupy the foremost place, not only because it supports and upholds us when we most require to be sustained, but because in this source of consolation there is something, we have reason to believe, of the Divine Spirit. . . ."

The "Wreck of the Golden Mary" brings out this truth very forcibly, in showing the chastened and softened feelings, with their outcome of patience and kindness, which the sufferings of the shipwrecked crew brought into play. It would seem to me that it needs no little spiritual enlightenment to image forth a narrative which shall deal with such critical mental conditions which this state involves, without offending our sense of possibilities, or doing violence to our religious instincts. There is nothing far-fetched, to those who have learned the lesson here sought to be conveyed, in the rapture of joy with which both boats' crews are represented to be infected when, after being separated seventy-two hours, they come in view of one another again—" a joy," we read, which " had something in a manner divine in it; each was so forgetful of individual suffering, in tears of delight and sympathy for the people in the other boat." So, where the roughest of the men are spoken of as softening under their miseries, and as being as considerate of the ladies, and as compassionate of the child, as the best of the crew; and when they listen to Mrs. Atherfield singing little Lucy to sleep, and beg her to sing again, which she does, ending with the evening hymn, and repeats it every night at sunset, the crew taking up the last line, and shedding tears when it is done, we recognise a truthful illustration of his previously-enunciated belief, that " the power of finding some germs of comfort in our hardest trials must ever occupy the foremost place," and that, in this source of consolation, " there is something of the Divine Spirit." How full of beautiful meaning, too, is the allusion, introduced as though merely casually, to the poor fellows making the motion of uncovering their already bare heads when little Lucy is buried. Another remarkable instance from this tale may be added, ere passing on to a still more corroborative evidence:—

" Twenty-seven nights and twenty-six days. We were in no want of rain-water, but we had nothing else. And yet, even now, I never turned my eyes upon a waking face but it tried to brighten before mine. Oh, what a thing it is, in a time of danger and in the presence of death, the shining of a face upon a face !

I have heard it broached that orders should be given in great new ships by electric telegraph. I admire machinery as much as any man, and am as thankful to it as any man can be for what it does for us. But it will never be a substitute for the face of a man, with his soul in it, encouraging another man to be brave and true. Never try it for that. It will break down like a straw."

The further evidence spoken of is to be found in *The Haunted Man*, which might have been written distinctly to enunciate the truth of the uses of adversity—this being the scheme of the whole story. It tells of one who, soured by early wrongs and consequent sorrows, accepts the alternative presented to him of losing his memory of those bitter recollections, and of working the like blessing (as he esteems it) on those with whom he comes in contact. The sequel is finely worked out. What he fondly imagines will be a blessing turns out to be a great curse—a source of gross selfishness and evil subversion of the nice adjustment of the All-wise. Wherever he goes, he succeeds only in eradicating those sympathies and mutual confidences which are the growth of a common relationship in the sorrows of mankind—the buds of that blessed fruit of righteousness whose full growth is universal love—and leaving only the noisome weeds of selfishness and resentment to chastisement, unhallowed by the sad but profitable experiences of earthly probation. He plumbs the depths of his error when he finds himself upon a par, in all that is best in his nature, with a wild, untaught little outcast, whose habits and intellect are not more than equal to the lower animals, and repents the foolishness of his choice. He is assisted to a full sense of his error by a humble Christian woman, and the plot reaches its climax in the following very beautiful sentiment :—

"'May I tell you,' said Milly, 'why it seems a good thing for us to remember wrong that has been done us?'

"'Yes.'

"'That we may forgive it.'

"'Pardon me, great Heaven,' said Redlaw, lifting up his eyes, 'for having thrown away Thine own high attribute.'"

It is interesting to observe the use Charles Dickens makes of the sanctifying uses of affliction to purify his characters, and develope the good of which their natures are susceptible. It takes the harsh experiences of Eden to chasten the waywardness of young Martin Chuzzlewit, and ruin and dishonour to bring Mr. Dombey to the true knowledge of his evil pride, and the realisation of the love he had so wickedly spurned from him. The thunderbolt of affliction works a wonderful metamorphosis in disconsolate Mrs. Gummidge, and makes a very heroine of her. "With failing health and heightening resolution," there grew in Little Nelly's bosom "blessed thoughts and hopes, which are the portion of few but the weak and drooping." Trotty Veck, in *The Chimes*, moaning over the irredeemable vices of the poor, and the inutility of their existence, passes through the inexorable chastisements of a terrible dream, in which he is shown that the poor and wretched, even the worst, are capable of some good, and have a rightful share in the working-out of Time's problem. And the moral of it all is, in Dickens's own words, in a letter projecting the plan of this story, "that he has his portion in the new year no less than any other man, and that the poor require a deal of beating out of shape before their human shape is gone." In *The Carol*, a similar process is adopted to rescue Scrooge from utter selfishness. Richard Carstone, beggared and robbed of his life's usefulness in the pursuit of a phantom, learns how ill he has requited the kindness of his cousin, and resolves, dying, to commence the world afresh. *Hard Times* is a tale of a harsh and repellant system of training exploded and shown in all its ugliness by domestic calamities, in the agony of which its upholder learns, as he could have learned no other way, how blind and stupid he has been in his own conceit. Little Dorrit learns true goodness of heart within the walls of a prison; and even Jingle is reformed at that last stage of his vagabond career. Sidney Carton, by the chastening influences of a love which he knows cannot be requited, gains the power, assisted by other hard lessons, to give himself a living sacrifice to that hopeless passion. Pip, in *Great Expectations*, only learns the worth of his true friends when he loses all his riches, which had hardened his heart against them. Eugene Wrayburn is converted by the results of his being brought to the very threshhold of death by attempted murder; and his rescuer, Lizzie Hexam, learns the wisdom that allotted her sphere of early life amidst the prowling vultures of the river, when she finds that that repellant training fitted her to be the instrument of rescuing the drowning and half-murdered victim. And in the same volume (*Our Mutual Friend*) Bella's love is tried and proved by a severe test, concocted and carried out by her dearest friends.

Sufficient has been indicated to point out a motive for profitable investigation, by which the above list may be greatly extended; and I should be happy could I know that its compilation might awaken an interest and prompt a curiosity to corroborate its particulars by reading the books in which they are detailed, in those whose compunctions have hitherto hindered them, or in those in whom interest has not yet been awakened.

Two other articles of Christian faith received recognition at his hands—Baptism and the Sanctity of the Sabbath.

A short time ago a certain ill-informed clergyman tabooed the public reading of a certain profane piece entitled "The Bloomsbury Christening," upon the grounds that it cast contempt upon a sacred ordinance of Christianity. "The Bloomsbury Christening" was written by Dickens, and will be found in the *Sketches by Boz*, where it may be read and judged by its own merits or demerits. Now, the fact is, that Charles Dickens never suggested a slur upon that or any ordinance of the Church of England in all his writings, and a sentence from the account of the christening of Paul Dombey will fully exonerate him from so baseless a charge :—

"It might have been well for Mr. Dombey if he had thought of his own dignity a little less, and had thought of the *great origin and purpose of the ceremony*, in which he took so formal and so stiff a part, a little more." (*Dombey and Son*, chapter v.)

This seems to be the right place to add his commendatory references to other portions of the Church Prayer Book. We have seen how Captain Ravender, in simple faith, recited his recollections of the burial service over the dead child. Very kindred in spirit is Captain Cuttle, stricken and afflicted by the news of Walter's supposed loss at sea, opening his prayer book at the burial service. "And reading softly to himself, in the little back-parlour, and stopping now and then to wipe his eyes, the Captain, in a true and simple spirit, committed Walter's body to the deep." (*Dombey and Son*, chapter xxxiii.) It is alluded to in the burial of Little Nell, and again at the burial of Betty Higden (*Our Mutual Friend*), and in the *Uncommercial Traveller* it is termed "the best of services." (Chapter xxvi.)

A graceful compliment is paid to our transatlantic brethren when he says he knows "how mindful they usually are, in America, of that beautiful passage in the Litany, which remembers all sick persons and young children." (*American Notes*, chapter vi.)

The following passage from *Oliver Twist* seems to speak of the good influence that the Sabbath services of the church had upon him even at that early period :—

"And when Sunday came, how differently the day was spent from any way in which he had ever spent it yet! and how happily too; like all the other days in that most happy time! There was the little church, in the morning, with the green leaves fluttering at the windows; the birds singing without; and the sweet-smelling air stealing in at the low porch, and filling the homely building with its fragrance. The poor people were so neat and clean, and knelt so reverently in prayer, that it seemed a pleasure, not a tedious duty, their assembling there together; and though the singing might be rude, it was real, and sounded more musical (to Oliver's ears at least) than any he had ever heard in church before." (Chapter xxxii.)

There is a chapter in the *Uncommercial Traveller* devoted to "City of London" churches, which is a mild satire upon their retention, and their formal programme, in their deserted condition. "Hidden and forgotten," he calls them, "like the tombs of the old citizens who lie beneath them and around them—monuments of another age." They do not seem to have impressed him with any more solemn feelings than were inspired by the tombs and the dusty old registers, containing that which made some hearts leap, or some tears flow, in their day, and the echoes they yield of the time "when the City of London really was London, when the 'prentices and trained bands were of mark in the state; when even the Lord Mayor himself was a reality. . . ." In one of these churches he found a congregation of twenty, in another fourteen, "not counting an exhausted charity school in a gallery, which had dwindled away to four boys and two girls." The clergyman of the latter is described as being of a "moist and vinous look, and eke the bulbous boots, of one acquainted with 'twenty port and comet vintages," and "of a prandial presence and a muffled voice," who, when a boy rushes out of church with a whoop that vibrates to the top of the tower, "only glances up, as having an idea that somebody has said Amen in the wrong place," and continues his steady jog-trot, like a farmer's wife going to market. He does all he has to do in the same easy way, and gives us a concise sermon, still like the jog-trot of the farmer's wife on a level road.

This reminds us of Arthur Clennam's first Sunday evening in London, after his return from his long sojourn abroad; and the description may be aptly termed Dickens's sentiments on what is called Sabbatarianism :—

"It was a Sunday evening in London—gloomy, close, and stale. Maddening church bells of all degrees of dissonance, sharp and flat, cracked and clear, fast and slow, made the brick-and-mortar echoes hideous. Melancholy streets, in a penitential garb of soot, steeped the souls of the people who were condemned to look at them out of windows, in dire despondency. In every thoroughfare, up almost every alley, and down almost every turning, some doleful bell was throbbing, jerking, tolling, as if the plague were in the city, and the dead-carts were going round. Everything was bolted and barred that could by possibility furnish relief to an overworked people. No pictures, no unfamiliar animals, no rare plants or flowers, no natural or artificial wonders of the ancient world—all *taboo* with that enlightened strictness, that the ugly South Sea gods in the British Museum might have supposed themselves at home again. Nothing to see but streets, streets, streets. Nothing to change the brooding mind, or raise it up. Nothing for the spent toiler to do but to compare the monotony of his seventh day with the monotony of his six days—think what a weary life he led, and make the best of it—or the worst, according to the probabilities.

"At such a happy time, so propitious to the interests of religion and morality, Mr. Arthur Clennam . . . sat in the windows of a coffee-house on Ludgate Hill. . . . Fifty thousand lairs surrounded him, where people lived so unwholesomely, that fair water put into their crowded rooms on Saturday night would be corrupt on Sunday morning; albeit my lord, their county member, was amazed that they failed to sleep in company with their butcher's meat. Miles of close wells and pits of houses, where the inhabitants gasped for air, stretched far away towards every point of the compass. Through the heart of the town a deadly sewer ebbed and flowed in the place of a fine fresh river. What secular want could the million or so of human beings, whose daily labour, six days in the week, lay among these Arcadian objects, from the sweet sameness of which they had no escape between the cradle and the grave—what secular want could they possibly have upon their seventh day? Clearly, they could want nothing but a stringent policeman.

" Mr. Arthur Clennam sat in the window of the coffee-house on Ludgate Hill, counting one of the neighbouring bells, making sentences and burdens of songs out of it in spite of himself, and wondering how many people it might be the death of in the course of a year. As the hour approached, its changes of measure made it more and more exasperating. At the quarter it went off into a condition of deadly-lively importunity, urging the populace, in a voluble manner, to Come to Church, Come to Church, Come to Church! At the ten minutes it became aware that the congregation would be scanty, and slowly hammered out in low spirits, They *won't* come, they *won't* come, they *won't* come! At the five minutes it abandoned hope, and shook every house in the neighbourhood for three hundred seconds, with one dismal swing per second, as a groan of despair.

" 'Thank Heaven!' said Clennam, when the hour struck, and the bell stopped.

" But its sound had revived a long train of miserable Sundays, and the procession would not stop with the bell, but continued to march on. 'Heaven forgive me,' said he, 'and those who trained me. How I have hated this day!'" (*Little Dorrit*, chapter iii.)

But that Charles Dickens had a high reverence for the Sabbath, rightly used, according to his ideas of right, I quote a passage from his *American Notes* to prove:—

" Next morning, when the sun was shining brightly, and the clear church bells were ringing, and sedate people in their best clothes enlivened the pathway near at hand and dotted the distant thread of road, there was a pleasant Sabbath peacefulness on everything, which it was good to feel. It would have been the better for an old church ; better still for some old graves ; but, as it was, a wholesome repose and tranquillity pervaded the scene, which, after the restless ocean and the hurried city, had a doubly grateful influence on the spirits." (Chapter v.)

Finally, a passage from *Dombey and Son* will close this part of my work :—

" Oh Saturdays ! Oh happy Saturdays, when Florence always came at noon, and never would, in any weather, stay away, though Mrs. Pipchin snarled and growled, and worried her bitterly. Those Saturdays were Sabbaths for at least two little Christians among all the Jews, and did the holy Sabbath work of strengthening and knitting up a brother's and a sister's love." (Chapter xii.)

The attention of the public has recently been called to a reprint of an early and almost forgotten brochure of Charles Dickens. It had been better had it been altogether forgotten, as, without an insight into the formation of his religious character, it is calculated to pronounce a very adverse judgment upon it. We cannot think, judging from the preceding quotations, that he himself would have consented willingly to its republication.

This brochure is entitled, *Sunday under three heads— As it is ; as Sabbath Bills would make it ; as it might be made*. It was originally published, under the *nom-de-plume* of Timothy Sparks, in 1836, the same year of the publication of *Sketches by Boz*, and exhibits very remarkably the crudeness and inexperience of youth, of which he speaks in the preface to that collection. It was dedicated to the Bishop of London, whose strictures on the subject of Sunday excursions had excited much animadversion, and it contained the severest criticism on the Sabbath bill of Sir Andrew Agnew, which certainly *was* an outrageous measure, proposing heavy penalties for working, opening shops and houses of entertainment, being present at public meetings or assemblies, letting or hiring carriages, travelling in steamboats, starting vessels on their voyages, etc., on Sundays.

This bill he repudiates as a mass of monstrous absurdity, and, from beginning to end, a piece of deliberate cruelty and crafty injustice, directed against the interests of the poor, by robbing them of their only day of recreation, and by forcing them into the hypocrisy of foregoing every pleasure which made that day acceptable to them, and making it one of austerity and gloom.

Here we have the honest and fearless expression of that sympathy for the poor which afterwards became one of the most powerful levers of his success as a writer; and had that comprised the scope of his argument, many earnest Christians might have been at one with him, and admitted the truth of his pleas, when he urged the necessity of a Sunday holiday in the country for the overworked and surfeited toilers of London. But when, with all his characteristic intense ardour, unrestrained in the recklessness, the impatience of contradiction, and the self-opinionativeness of youth, he goes to the most extravagant extremes, he severs the approbation of judicious Christians from his sweeping schemes, and utterly ruins the cause he advocates.

He depicts two imaginary (very imaginary) places of worship, in a very offensive style, in his description of "Sunday as it is." The first is a fashionable church, where a young clergyman of noble family and elegant demeanour reads the prayers in an impressive manner, hurrying nonchalently over the uncomfortable parts with a studied regard for the taste and feelings of his auditors, and is followed by a sleek divine, who murmurs, in a voice kept down by rich feeding, most comfortable doctrines for exactly twelve minutes. The second is a "stronghold of intolerant zeal and ignorant enthusiasm," where a coarse man of forbidding accent calls upon the sacred founder of the Christian faith in terms of disgusting and impious familiarity, and preaches so hideously about the horrors prepared for the wicked in a future state, that one of his congregation falls senseless from fear. These alone are presented as types of the Christian sanctuary, and presented in such a manner as to lead the reader to infer that they were sufficiently typical of *all* Sunday services, and a demonstration of his hostility to all, as a Puritanical hindrance of the enjoyment of the Sunday holiday. What a contrast to the sentiments of the matured Christian, who has written so much that is commendatory of the Sabbath and the sanctuary!

When he speaks of "Sunday as it might be made," he advocates, in the spirit of positively offensive contradiction to the scruples of the Bishop and his supporters, the encouragement of cricket, quoits, and other games on Sunday afternoons, the opening of museums and picture galleries; while, in "Sunday as it is," he applauds the custom of river and road excursions, and says, approvingly, that the taverns are crowded, the glass is circulated, and the joke goes round.

That all this is the rash impetuosity of inexperience and crude judgment, unendorsed in its most extravagant features by succeeding writings, is sufficient reason why "Sunday under three Heads" should not be admitted into the evidence of the *Religious Sentiments of Charles Dickens.*

CHAPTER VIII.

Charles Dickens a Christian Advocate

O far testimony has been adduced in support of Charles Dickens's faith in the doctrines of the Bible, and his unsparing castigation of those who, professing those doctrines, act contrary to the spirit of them. But it is desirable that it should be shown that he not merely *assented* to the teachings of Christianity, nor was but a nominal and conventional Christian, but had sufficiently grasped the spirit of the gospel to manifest it in advocacy.

The above remarks may be corroborated by the following:—

"The begging-letters flying about by every post, made it perfectly manifest that a set of lazy vagabonds were interposed between the general desire to do something to relieve the sickness and misery under which the poor were suffering, and the suffering poor themselves. That many who sought to do some little to repair the social wrongs, inflicted in the way of preventible sickness and death upon the poor, were strengthening those wrongs, however innocently, by wasting money on pestilent knaves cumbering society. . . . That the crowning miracle of the New Testament, after the miracle of the blind seeing, and the lame walking, and the restoration of the dead to life, was the *miracle* that the poor had the gospel preached to them. That while the poor were unnaturally and unnecessarily cut off by the thousand, in the prematurity of their age, or in the rottenness of their youth—for of flower or blossom such youth has none—the gospel was NOT preached to them, saving in hollow and unmeaning voices. That of all wrongs, this was the first mighty wrong the Pestilence (*i.e.*, the begging-letter pestilence) warned us to set right." (From *The Begging-letter Writer*.)

We have seen that he does not look to the Pardiggle method of righting this wrong as likely to be successful, with its cold-blooded professional system, and want of sympathy. We have seen how skilfully he has pointed a moral, in showing how the few heartfelt words and sympathetic action of Esther and Ada effected a response from people whom Mrs. Pardiggle's ministrations only provoked to angry retaliation and contempt. The truth thus insinuated is more particularly expressed in "Nobody's Story."

It is a story of one of an immense family, all of whose sons and daughters gained their daily bread by daily work, prolonged from their rising up betimes until their lying down at night, beyond which destiny he had no prospect, and sought none. His fireside was a bare one, all hemmed in by blackened sheets; his wife was old before her time, and her hands were hardened with toil; his children were stunted and unwholesome, but he had the poor man's love for all these objects, nevertheless. But the Bigwig family, who had undertaken to think for him, and manage his affairs, quarrelled concerning what it was lawful to teach his children, and while they quarrelled, he saw his family growing up in ignorance and evil. Moreover, the Bigwig family impounded his escape from his debasing surroundings on his Sundays, and closed the wonders of the world, the greatness of creation, the workings of nature, and the beauties of art to him. Then a pestilence broke out among the labourers, and slayed them by the thousands, and thus new poison was distilled into the always murky, always sickening air. He had no means of escape, and remained there to see his dear ones die.

A kind preacher came to console him, and this is how he replies to him :—

"Oh, what avails it, missionary, to come to me, a man condemned to residence in this fœtid place, where every sense bestowed upon me for my delight becomes a torment, and where every minute of my numbered days is new mire added to the heap under which I lie oppressed ! But, give me my first glimpse of heaven through a little of its light and air ; give me pure air ; help me to be clean ; lighten this heavy atmosphere and heavy life, in which our spirits sink, and we become the indifferent and callous creatures you too often see us ; gently and kindly take the bodies of those who die among us out of the small room where we grow to be so familiar with the awful change that even ITS sanctity is lost to us ; and then, teacher, then I will hear—none know better than you how willingly—of Him whose thoughts were so much with the poor, and who had compassion for all human sorrows !"

"Nobody's Story" is a very prominent example of that doctrine which Charles Dickens so consistently and fearlessly advocated, and which has had so much to do with his popularity and success. I mean, his great charity for the poor and lowly and oppressed, which the scripture emphasises as the highest of all Christian attributes, and which is referred to in this section as being more than a sentiment—as being a cause to which he devoted the strength of his genius, and of which he was pre-eminently an apostle. In the *Uncommercial Traveller* he introduces himself as travelling for the great house of Human Interest Brothers, and his books testify eloquently to the profitable business done for his principals. His religion was essentially the religion of humanity, as enunciated in Master Humphrey's will, of which the deaf gentleman says :—

"And as true charity not only covers a multitude of sins, but includes a multitude of virtues—such as forgiveness, liberal construction, gentleness and mercy to the faults of others, and the remembrance of our own imperfections and advantages—he bade us not inquire too closely into the venial errors of the poor, but finding that they *were* poor, first to relieve them, and then endeavour—at an advantage—to reclaim them." (*Master Humphrey's Clock.*)

To this may be added the supposed sentiments of Master Humphrey - in life (the real sentiments of Charles Dickens):—

" Heart of London, there is a moral in thy every stroke ! As I look on at thy indomitable working, which neither death, nor press of life, nor grief, nor gladness out of doors will influence one jot, I seem to hear a voice within thee which sinks into my heart, bidding me, as I elbow my way among the crowd, have some thought for the meanest wretch that passes, and, being a man, to turn away with scorn and pride from none that bear the human shape."

This was, indeed, no merely ethical article of Christian duty with the author. He preaches and enforces it at every opportunity. In *The Chimes* he says:—

" Whoever turns his back upon the fallen and disfigured of his kind, abandons them as vile ; and does not trace or track with pitying eyes the unfenced precipice by which they fell from good—grasping in their fall some tufts and shreds of that last soil, and clinging to them still when bruised and dying in the gulf below—does wrong to heaven and to man, to time and eternity."

It cannot fail to have been gathered, from many preceding quotations, that he held to the true scriptural faith that the most degraded soul was worth the seeking, and that he further insisted that in every sinner there was the germ of good, which it was possible to develope, though hidden and obscured by present bad influences and surroundings, which, in his own mind, form a strong plea for them, command his sympathies, and impel him to the strongest advocacy of their claim to the consideration of Christianity. Harshness and injustice to the unfortunate poor always stimulated him to anger, and many extracts might be cited to show how heartily he despised the fine talk about their depravity and incorrigibility, with which those who are beyond the reach of such demoralising influences pharisaically vaunt their own high standard of morality. Such, in effect, are his sentiments, of which the following, from the many, are striking examples:—

"Cant as we may, and as we shall to the end of all things, it is very much harder for the poor to be virtuous than the rich; and the good that is in them shines the brighter for it. In many a noble mansion lives a man, the best of husbands and of fathers, whose private worth in both capacities is justly lauded to the skies. But bring him here, upon this crowded deck. Strip from his fair young wife her silken dress and jewels, unbind her braided hair, stamp early wrinkles on her brow, pinch her pale cheeks with care and much privation, array her faded form in coarsely patched attire, let there be nothing but his love to set her forth or deck her out, and you shall put it to the proof indeed. So change his station in the world, that he shall see in those young things who climb about his knee: not records of his wealth and name: but little wrestlers with him for his daily bread; so many poachers on his scanty meal; so many units to divide his every sum of comfort, and further to reduce its small amount. In lieu of the endearments of childhood in its sweetest aspect, heap upon him all its pains and wants, its sicknesses and ills, its fretfulness, caprice, and querulous endurance; let its prattle be, not of engaging infant fancies, but of cold, and thirst, and hunger; and if his fatherly affection outlive all this, and he be patient, watchful, tender; careful of his children's lives, and mindful always of their joys and sorrows; then send him back to Parliament, and Pulpit, and to Quarter Sessions, and when he hears fine talk of the depravity of those who live from hand to mouth, and labour hard to do it, let him speak up, as one who knows, and tell those holders forth that they, by parallel with such a class, should be High Angels in their daily lives, and lay but humble siege to heaven at last." (*American Notes*, chapter xv.—" The Emigrant Ship.")

In *Dombey and Son* (chapter xlvii.), strongly emphasising the odiousness of the dens of the very poor, "at the lightest mention of which humanity revolts, and dainty delicacy, living in the next street, stops her ears, and lisps, ' I don't believe it!'" he continues :—

"And then, calling up some ghastly child, with stunted form and wicked face, hold forth on its unnatural sinfulness, and lament its being, so early, far away from heaven—but think a little of its having been conceived, and born, and bred in hell!

"Those who study the physical sciences, and bring them to bear upon the health of man, tell us that if the noxious particles that rise from vitiated air were palpable to the sight, we should see them lowering in a dense black cloud above such haunts, and rolling slowly on to corrupt the better portions of a town. But if the moral pestilence that rises with them, and, in the eternal laws of outraged nature, is inseparable from them, could be made discernible too, how terrible the revelation! Then should we see depravity, impiety, drunkenness, theft, murder, and a long train of nameless sins against the natural affections and repulsions of mankind, overhanging the devoted spots, and creeping on, to blight the innocent and spread contagion among the pure. Then should we see how the same poisoned fountains that flow into our hospitals and lazar-houses, inundate the jails, and make the convict-ships swim deep, and roll across the seas, and overrun vast continents with crime. Then should we stand appalled to know, that where we generate disease to strike our children down and entail itself on unborn generations, there also we breed, by the same certain process, infancy that knows no innocence, youth without modesty or shame, maturity that is mature in nothing but in suffering and in guilt, blasted old age that is a scandal on the form we bear. Unnatural humanity! When we shall gather grapes from thorns, and figs from thistles; when fields of grain shall spring up from the offal in the by-ways of our wicked cities, and roses bloom in the fat churchyards that they cherish; then may we look for natural humanity and find it growing from such seed.

"Oh for a good spirit who would take the housetops off, with a more potent and benignant hand than the lame demon in the tale, and show a Christian people what dark shapes issue from amidst their homes, to swell the retinue of the Destroying Angel as he moves among them! For only one night's view of the pale phantoms rising from the scenes of our too-long neglect; and from the thick and sullen air where vice and fever propagate together, raining the tremendous social retributions which are ever pouring down, and ever coming thicker! Bright and blest the morning that should rise on such a night; for men, delayed no more by stumbling-blocks of their own making, which are but specks of dust upon the path between them and eternity, would then apply themselves, like creatures of one common origin, owing one duty to the father of one family, and tending to one common end, to make the world a better place!

"Not the less bright and blest would that day be for rousing some who never have looked out upon the world of human life around them, to a knowledge of their own relation to it, and for making them acquainted with a perversion of nature in their own concentrated sympathies and estimates; as great, and yet as natural in its development, when once begun, as the lowest degradation known."

With him, human and personal sympathy, armed with the mercies inculcated in the gospel, was the great factor for human regeneration; and every one, he emphasised, however lowly and contracted their sphere of action, has lot and share in the great work. We have seen that he did not depreciate the sacredness and great usefulness of the ministerial office, honourably and righteously administered; but that he cordially assented to the Bible doctrine of the "priesthood of all believers," is inferred from the personal responsibility he fastens upon all Christian people to share the onerous of duty. The religion he admired was the religion whose faith was manifested by its works of mercy and charity, and such a character, especially when associated with lowliness of station and modesty of profession, was his standard of true Christianity. The portraiture of such a *beau ideal* is drawn in Joe Gargery, whom, in words put into the mouth of Pip, he calls "that good Christian man." The conduct which calls forth the eulogy is, that when Pip, who, in his prosperity has despised and turned his back upon his poor friend, has lost everything, and is lying ill and in extremity, Joe Gargery hastens to his bedside, and, without reproach or a hint of the past, nurses him with the tenderness and solicitude of a great love.

There is a notable instance of the fruits and reward of lowly Christianity in a piece of his called "A Walk in a Workhouse." In an insalubrious department known by the undignified name of the "Itch Ward," he found a flabby, raw-boned, untidy pauper nurse, crying, sobbing, and in deep and real grief and affliction, because of the death of a child which had been dropped in the street, and being brought in, had died an hour before his visit:—

"The dropped child seemed too small and poor a thing for death to be in earnest with, but death had taken it; and already its diminutive form was neatly washed, composed, and stretched as if in sleep upon a box. I thought I heard a voice from heaven saying, It shall be well for thee, O nurse of the itch ward, when some less gentle pauper does those offices to thy cold form, that such as the dropped child are the angels who behold My Father's face!"

In such lowly spheres has he found the truest and most untainted manifestations of true charity. "What the poor are to the poor," he writes, when telling the sad story of the bricklayers' wives in *Bleak House*, "is little known, excepting to themselves and God." When he comes to speak of the public administration of charity, he inveighs, with severe strictures, against its uncharitableness and want of sympathy; and speaking of it in one place (*The Chimes*), marks his disapprobation of it by saying it is not the charity once preached upon a mount. But it is through old Betty Higden, in *Our Mutual Friend*, that he enunciates his sentiments most strongly upon this matter. He shows her blazing with shame, and horror, and repugnance, when it is hinted to her that her foster-child should be removed to an institution; and he depicts her flying from the kindly bystander, who would urge her to go and see the parish doctor, like a hunted animal. With sufficient money sewn in the breast of her gown to pay for her burial, that she might die independent, and not a pauper, and knowing that her life was nearing its end, she stubbornly and resolutely goes on, trusting the Lord to see her through it, faring on and hiding, hiding and faring on, as though she were a murderess, and the whole country were up after her. In her wandering fancy she hears the tender river saying to her, "Come to me, come to me! When the cruel shame and terror you have so long fled from must beset you, come to me! I am the Relieving Officer appointed by eternal ordinance to do my work; I am not held in estimation according as I shirk it. My breast is softer than the pauper nurse's; death in my arms is peacefuller than among the pauper wards. Come to me!" Anon, she lights on the shameful spectacle of desolate creatures huddled together like vermin, while the appointed evader of the public trust did his dirty office of trying to weary them out, and so get rid of them. However tired, however footsore, she would start up and be driven away by the awakened horror of falling into the hands of charity. "It is a remarkable Christian improvement," he adds, "to have made a pursuing Fury of the Good Samaritan; but it was so in this case, and is a type of many, many, many." At length, sinking at the foot of a tree, which brought to her mind the foot of the Cross, she, committing herself to Him who died upon it, was thankful that she would be found dead by some of her own sort.

Observation teaching him that all this was true—and he learned it early enough, as *Oliver Twist* shows—there is no wonder, in the vigour of his convictions and the fearlessness of his championship of the Right, he should denounce it in the following words:—

"For when we have got things to the pass that, with an enormous treasure at disposal to relieve the poor, the best of the poor detest our mercies, hide their heads from us, and shame us by starving to death in the midst of us, it is a pass impossible of prosperity, impossible of continuance. . . . This boastful handiwork of ours, which fails in its terrors for the professional pauper, the sturdy breaker of windows, and the rampant tearer of clothes, strikes with a cruel and wicked stab at the stricken sufferer, and is a horror to the deserving and unfortunate. We must mend it, lords and gentlemen and honourable boards, or in its own evil hour it will mar every one of us." (*Our Mutual Friend*, book iii., chapter viii.)

A powerful lever for the elevation of the masses, in his opinion, was education, and it would have rejoiced his heart had he lived to see the day which came, when education, comprehensive and unsectarian, was recognised and adopted as the only safe principle to work on—substantially the words he used in a speech at the Birmingham Polytechnic Institution, in February 1844; adding that "no society could go on punishing men for preferring vice to virtue without giving them the means of knowing what virtue was." His sentiments on unsectarian education are still more boldly expressed in a letter addressed to and quoted by his biographer, where he speaks of having offered to describe the Ragged School, and where the following most characteristic words occur:—"I will give a description of them in a paper on education, if the *Review* is not afraid to take ground against the church catechism and other mere formularies and subtleties, in reference to the education of the young and ignorant." This was written in 1842, between the publication of *Martin Chuzzlewit* and the *Christmas Carol;* but it will be perceived that the same independent spirit pervades it which manifested itself in the latter end of his life, when he charged his children, in his will, to be guided by the teachings of the New Testament, and to put no faith in any man's narrow construction of its letter. Mr. Foster declares that the education of the very poor was a matter always nearest his heart.

Another matter inseparably bound up with religion is the promotion of temperance, and the friends of the now mighty movement will be glad to know what Charles Dickens had to say upon that subject, and glad to find that he has been much maligned thereon. A man subject to no violent extremes, he seems to have adopted a temperate view of the matter; and when we consider the habits of his day, and the position that temperance reform occupied then, I may venture to assert that he was a reformer in the truest sense, and gave no uncertain sound in his denunciation of the national vice, and displayed the greatest good sense in dealing with the matter. Ever consistent to the clearly defined principles by which he was actuated, he has the same remedy to prescribe for drunkenness, so far as the poor are concerned, as he elsewhere recommends for their redemption from the other evils and curses of their lot, as we read in the *Sketches:—*

"Gin-drinking is a great vice in England, but wretchedness and dirt are a greater; and until you improve the homes of the poor, or persuade a half-famished wretch not to seek relief in the temporary oblivion of his own misery, with the pittance which, divided among his family, would furnish a morsel of bread for each, gin shops will increase in number and splendour. If temperance societies would suggest an antidote against hunger, filth, and foul air, or could establish dispensaries for the gratuitous distribution of Lethe-water, gin palaces would be numbered among the things that were." (Chapter xxii.)

His views remained precisely the same twelve years after, when, in writing upon this subject, he defined true temperance reform to lie in bravely dealing with the physical and moral temptations which led the poor to the gin shop, and objected to temperance reform as then fulminated, because the gin shop itself was the object of attack, and these things were left out of account altogether. One observation in his letters upon the question is worth cogitating on:—" When a man shows so forcibly the side of the medal on which the people in their faults and crimes are stamped, he is the more bound to help us to a glance at that other side on which the faults and vices of the Government placed over the people are not less gravely impressed." The same reproach is emphasised in his criticism on Hogarth's celebrated picture, " Gin Lane," also included in the biography, where he says that he thinks it to be a remarkable trait in the picture that, " while it exhibits drunkenness in the most appalling forms, it also forces on attention a most neglected wretched neighbourhood, and an unwholesome, indecent, abject condition of life, that might be put as frontispiece to our sanitary report of a hundred years later date."

His attitude on the subject of temperance reform policy irresistibly reminds one of the story of the pump, which stood rusty, broken, and unused, and lost in the growth of weeds and accumulation of dirt around it, in a gentleman's back-garden. It occurred to that gentleman one day that it was a pity to see the pump, in itself an excellent and useful implement, so given over to ruin and decay; so he had the dirt and the weeds cleared away, the handle mended, the rust scraped off, and the whole structure repainted. But, alas! when all this was done, and the pump was set to work, there was nothing but filth could be pumped from it. The fountain was corrupt with neglect and rottenness, and though the pump looked very pretty, it was as useless as it was before. So Charles Dickens thought that a great deal of so-called temperance work succeeded in "painting the pump," while it left the source and fountain of the evil untouched; and when we read of Mr. Stiggins and Anthony Humm and the Brick Lane Branch temperance meeting, we must make allowances for his unflinching repudiation of pump-painters and surface reformers.

It may be objected that he fell into the somewhat common oversight of associating drunkenness with the lower classes only, without recognising that the vice was as pronounced in better society. It is true that there is a great deal of drinking going on throughout his books, that Mr. Pickwick and his friends are greatly too much addicted to punch and other strong liquors, and that that venerable old gentleman is represented as preserving his highly virtuous and benevolent disposition in the face of his occasional infirmity of being overcome by intoxication; that David Copperfield patronises the "genuine stunner" at an exceedingly tender age, without so much as a reprehension from his maturer self; and that so many of Dickens's lady-characters are surreptitiously partial to a sip of something strong; and that these shortcomings are represented as consistent with goodness and virtuous character, and harmless to their reputation. It is not my province to raise an objection, nor to gainsay the imputation: the fact remains that he was not impressed with the necessity of total abstinence as a method of discouraging drunkenness. But that he did not altogether lose sight of the painfully true fact, that the vice was to be found in the higher grades of society, is obvious from a remark made in his criticism of Hogarth's pictures, to the effect that Hogarth "was never disposed to spare the kind of drunkenness that was of more *respectable* engenderment, as one sees in his midnight modern conversation, the election plates, and crowds of stupid aldermen and other guzzlers." In *A Tale of Two Cities* he speaks of the great improvement time has brought about in drinking customs, thus indirectly stigmatising the intemperate habits of "good society" of a past day. We now are accustomed to look upon the days in which he himself wrote—at least the earlier of his books—as hard drinking days, and congratulate ourselves upon the still further improvement time has wrought in this respect—an improvement which, I doubt not, Charles Dickens, with his readiness to acknowledge all that was demonstrably good, would not fail to admit, were he amongst us now to give an opinion.

It must not be supposed that he wholly condemned the work of temperance societies, or failed to recognise the real worth of their efforts. He has something good to say of the great "pencil" of the temperance party—George Cruikshank—and in writing to Mr. Foster, he speaks of his remarkable work, *The Bottle*, as being "very powerful indeed—the last two plates admirable," though he qualifies his commendations with the conscientious objection that he thought the philosophy of the work all wrong, because, to be true, the evil should have begun in sorrow, or poverty, or ignorance.

A fair exposition of his sentiments on temperance agitation, as he knew it in his day, is to be found in his report of a Temperance Convention at Cincinnati, in the *American Notes* (chapter xi.), where he speaks kindly of a temperance procession, several thousands strong, with bands of music to boot, and banners out of number, as "a fresh, holiday-looking concourse altogether." He good-humouredly describes the proceedings, which seem to have somewhat amused him, though not disagreeably ; and he winds up by remarking that "the main thing was the conduct and appearance of the audience throughout the day, and that was admirable and full of promise."

Charles Dickens, then, did not look upon the drink problem from the teetotal platform; but from the point of view from which he did survey it, he was a staunch ally of all those who are pledged to the uprooting of the monster evil of drunkenness, and they would do well to learn many things out of his book, to strengthen their hands and to teach them how to get at the root of the matter.

No one knew better than he did what drink *could* do. There never was a more terrible picture painted of the work of strong drink than is included in the *Sketches*, under the title of "The Drunkard's Death." Let the following extracts bear witness:—

"Is there any man who has mixed much with society, or whose avocations have caused him to mingle, at one time or other, with a great number of people, who cannot call to mind the time when some shabby, miserable wretch, in rags and filth, who shuffles past him now in all the squalor of disease and poverty, was a respectable tradesman or clerk, or a man following some thriving pursuit, with good prospects, and decent means? or cannot any of our readers call to mind from among the list of their *quondam* acquaintance, some fallen and degraded man, who lingers about the pavement in hungry misery —from whom every one turns coldly away, and who preserves himself from sheer starvation, nobody knows how? Alas! such cases are of too frequent occurrence to be rare items in any man's experience; and but too often arise from one cause— drunkenness—that fierce rage for the slow, sure poison, that oversteps every other consideration; that casts aside wife, children, friends, happiness, and station; and hurries its victims madly on to degradation and death."

He sat by the dying bed of his wife, having reeled home from the tavern in time to see her die. "She alone had clung to him in good and evil, in sickness and poverty, and how had he rewarded her?"

"He rushed from the house, and walked swiftly through the streets. Remorse, fear, shame, all crowded on his mind. Stupefied with drink, and bewildered with the scene he had just witnessed, he re-entered the tavern he had quitted shortly before. Glass succeeded glass. His blood mounted, and his brain whirled round. Death! Every one must die, and why not *she?* She was too good for him; her relations had often told him so. Curses on them! Had they not deserted her, and left her to whine away the time at home? Well—she was dead, and happy perhaps. It was better as it was. Another glass—one more! Hurrah! It was a merry life while it lasted; and he would make the most of it."

Time goes on—his sons desert him, and run riot in a life of crime—one of them he, in his intoxication, betrays into the hangman's hands—his daughter flies from him, and with her his means of livelihood. He begs his bread, and spends a year partly in jail and partly in the open air, houseless and vagrant; but when he sinks down at last, in the last stage of poverty and disease, he is a drunkard still. Then the horrible accusations of conscience assail him—the inevitable retribution that Dickens so firmly believed in—and in a state of frenzy he ends his shameful career in the river. Unrecognised and unpitied, his swollen and disfigured body is borne to the grave, and "there it has long since mouldered away."

In *Hard Times* there is an uncompromising and emphatic testimony to the power of drink, in the delineation of the degraded wife of Stephen Blackpool. In Stephen's words, "She were a young lass—pretty enow—wi' good accounts of herseln," when he married her; but he tells, in plain, unmistakable terms, of how she trod the wretched road that so many like her *have* trod—how he had gone home— twenty times!—and found all he had in the world vanished, and her, without a sense left to bless herself, lying on bare ground—how she left him, disgraced herself, and coom back—coom back—coom back. How he paid her to keep away, and how, five years elapsing, she had come back again. And this is how the author describes her:—

"Such a woman! A disabled, drunken creature, barely able to preserve her sitting posture by steadying herself with one begrimed hand on the floor, while the other was so purposeless in trying to push away her tangled hair from her face, that it only blinded her the more with the dirt upon it. A creature so foul to look at, in her tatters, stains, and splashes, but so much fouler than that in her moral infamy, that it was a shameful thing even to see her.

"After an impatient oath or two, and some stupid clawing of herself with the hand not necessary to her support, she got her hair away from her eyes sufficiently to obtain a sight of him. Then she sat swaying her body to and fro, and making gestures with her unnerved arm, which seemed intended as the accompaniment to a fit of laughter, though her face was stolid and drowsy." (Book ii., chapter x.)

Again, the abject father of the doll's dressmaker in *Our Mutual Friend*, who sells his daughter's confidence for five shillings, and straightway spends it all in drink, and Mr. Wickfield, in *David Copperfield*, the victim of a craving for wine, are striking examples of the fascination of strong drink, and warnings pointed enough, one would imagine, to bring home the sense of danger to those who are treading in their footsteps, and, as such, additions to the arguments of temperance reform.

A strong feature in his direct advocacy of the truths of religion is his realisation of its evidences in nature. He had grasped the great truth, that the "invisible things of Him since the creation of the world are clearly seen, being understood by the things that are made." This species of evidence has always held a prominent place in the argument for religion, and to those who value its advantage as a witness, the Christian evidences of Charles Dickens are commended.

In the human hand he saw such an evidence, and in *Dombey and Son* he says :—

" Long may it remain in this mixed world a point not easy of decision, which is the more beautiful evidence of the Almighty's goodness—the delicate fingers that are formed for sensitiveness and sympathy of touch, and made to minister to pain and grief, or the rough, hard, Captain Cuttle hand, that the heart teaches, guides, and softens in a moment ! " (Chapter xlix.)

In *Hard Times* a notable argument for the truth may be culled :—

" Stephen bent over his loom, quiet, watchful, and steady. A special contrast, as every man was in the forest of looms where Stephen worked, to the crashing, smashing, tearing piece of mechanism at which he laboured. Never fear, good people of an anxious turn of mind, that Art will consign Nature to oblivion. Set anywhere, side by side, the work of God and the works of man ; and the former, even though it be a troop of hands of very small account, will gain in dignity from the comparison." (Book ii., chapter xi.)

His enthusiasm in the wonders of creation was unbounded, and its most admirable feature was that he was not a mere nature-worshipper, but found in the excellency of these things a powerful motive for worshipping the Creator. Such was the lesson he learned, for instance, from that theme which has inspired so many pens— Niagara. Its vague immensity at first bewildered him, but, he continues—

" When I felt how near to my Creator I was standing, the first effect, and the enduring one—instant and lasting—of the tremendous spectacle, was Peace, Peace of mind, tranquillity, calm recollections of the Dead, great thoughts of Eternal Rest and Happiness : nothing of gloom or terror. . . . What voices spoke from out the thundering water ; what faces, faded from the earth, looked out upon me from its gleaming depth ; what heavenly promise glistened in those Angels' tears, the drops of many hues, that showered around, and twined themselves about the gorgeous arches which the changing rainbows made!" (*American Notes*, chapter xiv.)

In *Dombey and Son* he speaks of the sun rising and shedding, with its beams, the light of revelation upon man's heart:—

"So awful, so transcendent in its beauty, so divinely solemn. As he (Carker) cast his eyes upon it, where it rose, tranquil and serene, unmoved by all the wrong and wickedness on which its beams had shone since the beginning of the world, who shall say that some weak sense of virtue upon earth, and its reward in heaven, did not manifest itself, even to him?" (Chapter lv.)

In another place (*Martin Chuzzlewit*) he speaks of the religious influences of a deep forest glade on a glorious summer evening, and bewails the state of those who are dead to these holy influences, in saying that Tigg had never read the lessons these things conveyed.

Such another instance of the spiritual influence of nature is in the *Old Curiosity Shop*, where Nelly and her grandfather pass into a deep, shady wood, where, as they advance, serenity and cheerfulness steal upon them, for they feel that the tranquil mind of God is there, and sheds its peace upon them. (Chapter xxiv.)

Chapter xvi. of *Edwin Drood* concludes thus:—

"But Mr. Grewgious' . . . gaze wandered from the windows to the stars, as if he would have read in them something that was hidden from him. Many of us would, if we could; but none of us so much as know our letters in the stars yet—or seem likely to do it, in this state of existence—and few languages can be read until their alphabets are mastered."

It has already been noticed how Christmas inspired him with a strong faith in the memories and testimonies it bore along with it, and the peroration to a little piece called "A

Christmas Tree" may be advantageously added to former extracts on the subject :—

"Among the later toys and fancies hanging there—as idle often and less pure—be the images once associated with the sweet old waits, the softened music in the night, ever unalterable! Encircled by the social thoughts of Christmas-time, still let the benignant figure of my childhood stand unchanged! In every cheerful image and suggestion that the season brings, may the bright star that rested above the poor roof be the star of all the Christian world! A moment's pause, O vanishing tree, of which the lower boughs are dark to me as yet, and let me look once more! I know there are blank spaces on thy branches, where eyes that I have loved have shone and smiled; from which they are departed. But, far above, I see the raiser of the dead girl and the widow's son ; and God is good! If age be hiding for me in the unseen portion of thy downward growth, O may I, with a grey head, turn a child's heart to that figure yet, and a child's trustfulness and confidence."

Finally, there remains a piece amongst his miscellaneous writings, which would be most faithfully described as a tract. It is called "The Long Voyage," and has already been alluded to as containing the affecting incident of the little child, who was cared for by the ship's carpenter and the steward in the desert. Other instances of travel are enumerated, and gradually lead up to " thoughts of another kind of travel," of a voyager unexpectedly summoned from home, to a great distance, from whence he could never return, and where he suffered under bitter anguish and self-reproach because of his helplessness to set right what he had left wrong, and to do what he had left undone ; and thus the moral is pointed, and the whole design of the writing culminated, in the lesson that such a journey lies before us at the end of life, and such regrets will be the portion of those who neglect their Christian duty.

CHAPTER IX.

On Charles Dickens's Use of the Scriptures and Scriptural Doctrines throughout his Works.

MY work will be the more complete if I devote this chapter to a review of his use of and reference to the Scriptures and their doctrines throughout his works, in their consecutive order. Although this will be in the main part a *resumé*, yet it cannot fail to be advantageous to have the evidence focussed in order to an easy reference and continuous review, showing his habitual reverence for the Bible, and the development and growth of his confidence and faith in its teachings.

SKETCHES BY BOZ. The old lady of "Our Parish" sits of an evening with an open Bible on the table, and her maid regularly reads two or three chapters in the parlour aloud. Answered prayer is spoken of in the tale of the "Black Veil." The Almighty's prerogative of mercy and forgiveness, on repentance, is alluded to in "A Visit to Newgate."

PICKWICK PAPERS (1836). Answered prayer and repentance is spoken of in the clergyman's story.

OLIVER TWIST (1837). The mercy of God is relied on by Mrs. Maylie and Nancy.

NICHOLAS NICKLEBY (1838). Immortality is mentioned

in the case of the dying Smike, and Cheeryble speaks of Heavenly wisdom.

THE OLD CURIOSITY SHOP (1840). Immortality occupies a conspicuous place in this book, and the merciful provisions of God are much dwelt on.

BARNABY RUDGE (1841). The Bible is for the first time alluded to by name, under the title of the "Everlasting Book" (chapter xxv.), and men of gloom and austerity are bidden to read therein its contradiction of their doctrine. The Day of Judgment, the wrath of God (in the case of the murderer Rudge), the merciful dispensations of God, and prayer are all assented to.

AMERICAN NOTES (1842) contains the first mention of Jesus Christ, in two passages : 1. Commended to gloomy professors as the Great Master whose teachings they pervert; 2. As the Saviour of the world, who was mocked by the soldiery. The Day of Judgment is threatened to the upholders of slavery; and chapter xiv. concludes with a direct reference to the opening verses of the Scriptures:— "That first flood before the deluge—Light—came rushing on Creation at the word of God." Niagara is an evidence to him of God's greatness and love.

MARTIN CHUZZLEWIT (1843). With the exception of "Ruth in prayer," but one paragraph contains (two) allusions to the Bible. Woman is spoken of as God-beloved in old Jerusalem, and as bearing evidence against us on the Day of Judgment.

A CHRISTMAS CAROL (1843). Jesus Christ calling the little children to Him, and the star which guided the wise men to His birthplace, comprise the scriptural allusions in this Christmas story.

THE CHIMES (1844) contrasts the spirit of the Sermon on the Mount with the dispensation of charity as carried out by the disciples of its Preacher. Herein, too, is that remarkable type of the Resurrection of the body quoted in chapter vi., and a denunciation of those who have broken and flawed the Tables of the Law.

DOMBEY AND SON (1846) speaks of the Bible as the "eternal book for the weary and heavy laden," and the "blessed history," and goes on to eulogise Jesus Christ as "Him who had sweet compassion for, and interest in its every scene and stage, its every sorrow and suffering." Alice Marwood dies murmuring the sacred name. The one repentant sinner among the ninety-nine just men is spoken of; and Captain Cuttle reads the Sermon on the Mount on Sunday nights, "with as reverent an understanding of its heavenly spirit as if he had got it all by heart in Greek, and had been able to write any number of fierce theological disquisitions on its every phrase." Florence prays to the Father who does not despise His children's love. Immortality is endorsed, and God spoken of as working changes in the hearts He has made. Here also occurs the only thoughtful allusion in his writings to Baptism. The touch of Florence's hand on Edith Granger is said to be "like the prophet's rod of old upon the rock." The rising sun is spoken of as an evidence of religion.

THE BATTLE OF LIFE (1846) speaks of man being made in the image of God.

THE HAUNTED MAN (1848) illustrates an article of Christian faith, and speaks of forgiveness as the highest of Heaven's attributes. It contains several prayers, which address God as Father, and include two invocations of Jesus Christ.

DAVID COPPERFIELD (1850) presents us with a model Christian man in Daniel Peggotty, bringing out his reliance on God in the time of his trouble. Mrs. Gummidge quotes the promise, "As you have done it unto one of the least of these, you have done it unto Me." There are brief but assenting allusions to the Resurrection, the Judgment Day, and Immortality.

BLEAK HOUSE (1851). Esther and Ada comfort the bereaved mother by telling her what our Saviour said of children. Mr. Snagsby is reminded of the infant Jesus. Jo dies repeating the Lord's Prayer. The New Testament history is called interesting and affecting, and as having eloquence enough, if handled in simple reverence, to reach the lowest natures.

HARD TIMES (1854). Rachel cites Christ's compassion for the adulteress, and encourages Stephen in the hope of Immortality, who dies looking unto Jesus. The work of the Creator and the work of man are compared, to the exaltation of the former. The "last trump" is mentioned.

SEVEN POOR TRAVELLERS (1854) quotes the Angels' Song heard by the shepherds, the miracle on the widow's son of Nain, the barren fig-tree, Mary and the risen Saviour, Christ preaching from the ship and walking on the sea, and the people laying their sick where the shadows of the apostles might fall upon them; and speaks of God as the Divine Forgiver of injuries.

LITTLE DORRIT (1855). The true teaching of the New Testament is insinuated by force of contrast with the gloomy and hard creed of Mrs. Clennam, and by Little Dorrit's rebuke of her, in which she tells her to be guided by Jesus Christ. The New Testament is called a beneficent history. The Fatherhood of God, the Judgment, and Immortality are alluded to.

THE WRECK OF THE GOLDEN MARY (1856) mentions a prayer made in the name of Christ; records the simple, touching, and reverential prayer with which the captain buries the child, in which the love and life-giving power of Christ are extolled; and exhibits the castaways supported by religious faith through all their privations.

TALE OF TWO CITIES (1857). John xi. 25 is quoted *in extenso* three times, as the actuating principle by which Sidney Carton is nerved to his great sacrifice. Prayerful reliance on God is characteristic of Lucie Darnay, and in connection with her child, Christ blessing little children is spoken of. Immortality is spoken of.

UNCOMMERCIAL TRAVELLER (1859). The New Testament is eulogised (and quoted) as containing the most sublime history conceivable, which is better to read well, and let it speak, than to speak to an audience without tact. Matthew xxvi. 30 is alluded to. In the "Wreck of the Royal Charter" the resurrection is treated as an unquestionable fact, and the picture of an approved Christian minister is drawn.

GREAT EXPECTATIONS (1860). "Those noble passages" are spoken of, which remind humanity how it brought nothing into the world and can take nothing out, and how it fleeth like a shadow and never continueth long in one stay. The Judgment is alluded to. Pip prays, "Lord, be merciful to him, a sinner," at the death-bed of Magwitch.

OUR MUTUAL FRIEND (1864). The New Testament is termed the "sublime history," and "the beautiful coming to the Sepulchre" is spoken of. Betty Higden, dying, commends herself to Him who died on the Cross. God is alluded to as the Builder of the universe, who will shake its foundation.

EDWIN DROOD (1870) speaks of God as the Searcher of hearts, and alludes to the Resurrection.

Of his minor productions, the "Child's Dream of a Star" and the "Long Voyage" are strictly religious lessons. The "Begging-letter Writer" contains a reference to the Judgment, and reflects on Christianity for withholding the gospel from the poor. "Nobody's Story" tells how the poor will best be reached by the gospel; and "A Walk in a Workhouse" tells of the reward which shall be given to the compassionate nurse of the itch ward. "A Christmas Tree" ends with a testimony to the love of Christ, the Raiser of the dead, and a committal of himself to His mercy.

THE CHILD'S HISTORY OF ENGLAND (1853) speaks of the power of God over life and death, in the case of Canute; alludes to Christ as the healer of the sick, and to the lesson of the widow's mite; and teaches that faith is the principle of salvation.

I purposely remove this book from its chronological order, and place it at the end of the list, because it in a manner seals and attests the evidence by extolling the "great work of the Reformation" (chapter xxxi.), " which made England free" (*ibid*), and by speaking of the "inestimable service" which Miles Coverdale did the people by translating the Bible into English. (Chapter xxviii.)

In a letter written to a clergyman in 1856, quoted in the biography, he says of himself, that " there cannot be many men, I believe, who have a more humble veneration for the New Testament, or a more profound conviction of its all-sufficiency, than I have." Again, he writes in 1870, in reply to a suggestion that certain words in the tenth chapter of *Edwin Drood*—namely, "the highly popular lamb who has so long and unresistingly been led to the slaughter"—were open to misconstruction :—" It would be quite inconceivable to me, but for your letter, that any reasonable reader could possibly attach a scriptural reference to that passage. . . I am truly shocked. . . . I have always striven in my writings to express veneration for the life and lessons of our Saviour; *because I feel it.*" He alludes, in the same letter, to his having re-wrote the New Testament history for his children's advantage; and in his will we have seen how he again commended them to follow its teachings. This may well be supplemented by a selection from a letter written to his youngest son, on his leaving home to join his brother in Australia, which will both accurately define the religious convictions of the great author, and form a fitting conclusion to the evidence adduced from his writings :—

... "Try to do to others as you would have them do to you, and do not be discouraged if they fail sometimes. It is much better for you that they should fail in obeying the greatest rule laid down by our Saviour than that you should. I put a New Testament among your books for the very same reasons, and with the very same hopes, that made me write an easy account of it for you when you were a little child. *Because it is the best book that ever was, or will be, known in the world;* and because it teaches you the best lessons by which any human creature, who tries to be truthful and faithful to duty, can possibly be guided. As your brothers have gone away, one by one, I have written to each such words as I am now writing to you, and have entreated them all to guide themselves by this Book, putting aside the interpretations and inventions of man. You will remember that you have never at home been harassed about religious observances, or mere formalities. I have always been anxious not to weary my children with such things before they are old enough to form opinions respecting them. You will therefore understand the better that I now most solemnly impress upon you the truth and beauty of the Christian religion, as it came from Christ Himself, and the impossibility of your going far wrong if you humbly but heartily respect it. Only one thing more on this head. The more we are in earnest as to feeling it, the less we are disposed to hold forth about it. Never abandon the wholesome practice of saying your own private prayers, night and morning. I have never abandoned it myself, and I know the comfort of it."

A more fitting conclusion could not be found to my task than the tribute which was paid by the Bishop of Manchester, in Westminster Abbey, three days after Charles Dickens's death :—

"He has been called in one notice an apostle of the people. I suppose it is meant that he had a mission, but in a style and fashion of his own ; a gospel, a cheery, joyous, gladsome message, which the people understood, and by which they could hardly help being bettered; for it was the gospel of kindliness, of brotherly love, of sympathy in the widest sense of the word. I am sure I have felt in myself the healthful spirit of his teaching. Possibly we might not have been able to subscribe to the same creed in relation to God, but I think we would have subscribed to the same creed in relation to man. He who has taught us our duty to our fellow-men better than we knew it before, who knew so well to weep with them that wept, and to rejoice with them that rejoiced; who has shown forth in all his knowledge of the dark corners of the earth how much sunshine may rest upon the lowliest lot; who had such an evident sympathy with suffering, and such a natural instinct of purity, that there is scarcely a page of the thousands he has written which might not be put into the hands of a little child, must be regarded by those who recognise the diversity of the gifts of the spirit as a teacher sent from God. He would have been welcomed as a fellow-labourer in the common interests of humanity by Him who asked the question, 'If a man love not his brother whom he hath seen, how can he love God whom he hath not seen?'"

Printed by WALTER SCOTT, "*The Kenilworth Press,*" *Felling, Newcastle.*

www.ingramcontent.com/pod-product-compliance
Lightning Source LLC
Chambersburg PA
CBHW031455160426
43195CB00010BB/988